Cocktail Heaven

Cocktail
Heaven

Ed. Anna Southgate

© 2009 Kerswell Farm Ltd

This edition published by Kerswell Books Ltd

Printed 2009

This book is distributed in the UK by
Parkham Books Ltd
Kerswell Farm,
Parkham Ash, Bideford
Devon, England
EX39 5PR

enquiries@parkhambooks.co.uk

ISBN: 978-1-906239-01-5

DS0206. Cocktails

Creative Director: Sarah King
Designer: Paul Stewart-Reed & Phoebe Gibb
Photography: Paul Stewart-Reed

Printed in Singapore

1 3 5 7 9 10 8 6 4 2

contents

Introduction

Drinking has been a popular pastime for thousands of years, and the practice of mixing drinks – whether it be juices with water or other spirits and liqueurs – is probably just as ancient. We may associate cocktails with the 20th century but, by definition, a cocktail is a blend of two or more different drinks, so the very first one may well have been made by the ancient Egyptians, Greeks or Romans (although their motives may well have had more to do with creating health-imparting elixirs!)

The first documented mixed drink dates from the Middle Ages, with the 14th-century 'bragget'. This was a mix of mead (a honey-based liqueur still made in parts of England) and ale. In fact, several of the liqueurs used in cocktails today – Benedictine and Chartreuse, for example – date from the late Middle Ages, when they were created by monks, traditionally herbalists and apothecaries, who administered to the sick with their medicinal tinctures and elixirs. While the Europeans can be credited with developing the complex distillation, maceration and infusion techniques for making the spirits used in cocktails today, there is no doubt that the 'cocktail' was an American invention, the word first appearing in an American dictionary of 1803.

Defined as a 'mixed drink of spirit, bitters and sugar', the precise origins of the word 'cocktail' are hotly debated: some say it derives from the red cock's feather worn in the hats of the big winners on the gambling boats of the

Mississippi. Others insist that it originated with Betsy Flanagan, who served chicken dinners to American and French soldiers fighting in the Revolutionary War and after-dinner drinks decorated with the bird's tail feathers to shouts of *'Vive le cock tail!'* Yet others claim that it was French Creole apothecary, Antoine Peychaud, who gave us the word: during the 1790s in New Orleans, he measured out the spirits for his medicines in a *cocquetier* (an egg cup).

Whatever their origins, the craze for such fabulous concoctions soon became wider spread than the US. In 1923 cocktail-barman *extraordinaire,* Harry MacElhone, opened Harry's New York Bar in Paris. It was here that the 'bloody Mary' originated, along with many other classic cocktail creations. The passion for cocktails did not even abait during the Prohibition years. Americans who could afford to travel sought their favourite drinks in Europe, skipped across the border to Mexico or found solace in the Caribbean. For those who didn't travel, there were a good number of bootleggers and illegal bathtub stills supplying a pretty regular and plentiful volume of booze.

The fact that some of this home-grown alcohol was a little unrefined did nothing to hinder the continued success of the cocktail: in fact, cocktail-barmen became more ingenious and better inspired to create new concoctions in order to disguise the 'rough' nature of the spirits. The 1920s and the 1930s were truly the golden age of the cocktail, and their popularity has not diminished since that time. Generations of drinkers, inspired by foreign travel and new tastes, have encouraged the creation of new drinks – often with some quite outrageous names and combinations. Such is the nature of the cocktail – a whole lot of fun in a glass – that you can get away with asking a complete stranger for a 'slow, comfortable screw up against a wall', some 'sex on the beach' and even requesting the 'manager's daughter'!

cocktail basics

Anyone can make a cocktail – you do not have to be a pro! But, as with any 'art', it helps to have the right tools to do the job well.

measures

Quantities for the recipes in this book are given as measures. The word 'measure' is used because there is a slight variation between metric, British imperial and US measurements (each side of the Atlantic has a variation on the fluid ounce). Since most of the classic cocktails were invented in America, the 'jigger' used in bars in the United States is often a common measurement. It doesn't matter what 'jigger' you use – it could be a shot glass or an egg cup, for example – as long as you make sure that you use the same measure throughout so that the ratios of one spirit to another in any drink will be correct. It is not a bad idea to measure the total quantities of a drink in water before starting, to make sure that all of the ingredients fit in the glasses you have chosen for it! Remember, however, that shaking, stirring and blending with ice will dilute, and therfore, increase the volume of your finished drink.

ice

A cocktail is not a cocktail without ice. This is a vital ingredient, it is important that you don't skimp on it. Recipes vary, but you will almost certainly need ice cubes, broken ice or crushed ice. The object is almost to freeze the drink, while breaking down and combining the ingredients.

Broken ice is easy to make: simply put some whole ice cubes into a clean, polythene bag and hit them once or twice with a rolling pin! The aim is to break each ice cube into three pieces. For crushed ice, keep going with the rolling pin, or put broken ice into a blender. Most blenders available today can do this, and some make a feature of their ice-crushing abilities. Ice melts quickly, so do not make broken and crushed iced until you need it, and chill the drinking glasses before making the cocktail.

chilling glasses

There are three ways to make glasses cold:

1 Place them in a fridge or freezer for a couple of hours before use. Do not do this with fine crystal glasses, however, as they may shatter.

2 Fill the glasses with crushed ice before use. Always discard the ice and shake out any remaining water before pouring in the drink.

3 Fill the glasses with cracked ice and stir it around a little before discarding it. Pour in the drink immediately.

mixing terminology

For recipes that involve adding cocktail ingredients to a shaker, glass or blender, it is a good idea to put the cheapest ingredients in first! Start with lemon or lime juice, sugar syrup and fruit juices, then add the more valuable spirits and liqueurs. This way, if you make a mistake, the chances are that you only waste the less expensive ingredients.

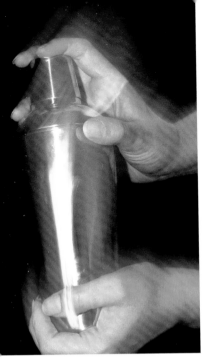

Whenever you are instructed to 'shake and strain' a cocktail, half-fill the shaker with clean ice cubes, add the ingredients and shake briskly, until the outside of the shaker feels very cold. Quickly pour the liquid through the strainer and into the glass, leaving the ice behind. Discard the ice. The volume of liquid will have increased because some of the ice will have melted and blended with the other ingredients in the cocktail. Remember to bear this in mind when making the drink as it may affect the size of glass that you choose.

Never shake and strain a drink with crushed ice: the ice will simply lodge in the strainer holes, clogging them up. A drink shaken with crushed ice is poured 'unstrained' into a glass. When instructed to 'shake and pour unstrained', add a glassful of ice to the shaker, pour in the ingredients and shake. Pour the drink into the same size of glass that you used to measure the ice.

When instructed to 'stir and strain' a cocktail, you should half-fill the mixing glass, or the bottom half of the shaker, with ice cubes, add the remaining ingredients and stir the drink with a long-handled bar spoon for at least 10 to 15 seconds. Then you can quickly strain the drink into your chosen glass using either a Hawthorn strainer (see page 12), the strainer part of your shaker or a fine-mesh sieve.

When instructed to 'stir and pour unstrained', repeat the process above, but only use a glassful of ice and don't strain the liquid after stirring. Add of all the contents to a glass the same size as the one that you used to measure the ice.

When instructed to 'build' a cocktail, you will create the drink directly in the glass in which it is served. Some drinks are built 'over ice', which means that the ice cubes go into the glass first and the liquors follow. Other drinks are made as a 'pousse-café'. A pousse-café relies on the difference in the 'weight' of liqueurs and spirits so that one sits on top of another in separate, often coloured, layers. This may take some practice, but the results are often spectacular. The key to success is to pour the liquids very slowly over the back (the rounded side) of a small spoon, or down the twisted stem of a long-handled bar spoon. This way, there is a good chance that each new layer will sit on top of the previous layer.

When making any cocktail, it is vital that you pour the drink as soon as you have made it or it will 'wilt' (become too diluted with melted ice). In some instances, a cocktail may separate into its component parts.

When using a 'twist of lemon, lime or orange peel', first rub a narrow strip of peel around the rim of the glass to deposit citrus oil on it. Then twist the peel so that the oil – usually one very small drop – falls into the drink. In some recipes, you may also drop the peel into the glass, while in others, you will be instructed to discard it.

A 'sugar-', 'salt-' or 'coconut-' rimmed glass is prepared by moistening the rim with a little lemon or lime juice and then dipping it into either sugar, salt or coconut.

equipment

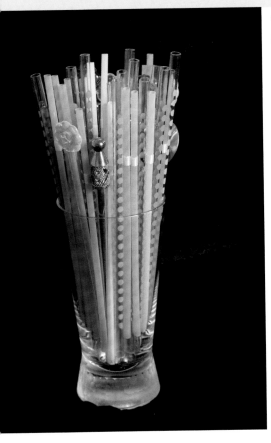

You may find that you already have some of the items listed below in your kitchen – and it is always possible to improvise. At the very least, you will need three basic pieces of equipment for making cocktails: a mixing glass, a shaker and a blender.

You use a mixing glass for drinks that require stirring before being poured, or strained, into the drinking glass. 'Professional' mixing glasses are designed for use with a Hawthorn strainer, but the bottom section of a standard shaker works just as well. You can also use a glass jug for mixing ingredients, pouring the drink through a fine-mesh sieve when ready to serve.

You have the choice of two kinds of shaker. A standard one comes with a built-in strainer, and is very convenient and easy to use. It is particularly good for drinks made with egg, cream, sugar syrup and fruit, which are strained to remove any bits of ice or fruit that may spoil the look of the drink. A Boston shaker has two flat-bottomed cones: one fits into the other. The liquid needs to be strained through a Hawthorn strainer, designed to fit over one of the cones.

A blender is best suited for making drinks using crushed ice, fresh fruit, ice cream and milk. The aim is to produce a drink with a milkshake-like consistency, so remember that too much blending will dilute the drink as crushed ice melts very quickly. It is also good to use blender if you are making up a large batch of drinks. (A good tip when serving a large batch of the same drink is to set the glasses in a row. Fill each glass by half first, then back-track until the blender jug is empty. That way, everyone gets the same amount of drink, all thoroughly mixed.)

equipment

Additional equipment:

Glasses

Tin- and bottle-opener/corkscrew

Long-handled bar spoon

Small, sharp paring knife for cutting garnishes

Measuring spoon for 'dry' sugar

Jigger, or chosen measure

Ice bucket and tongs

Cocktail sticks/toothpicks

Assorted straws, swizzle sticks/stirrers, muddlers

glasses

It is important to use the right glass for each drink, as this adds to the visual impact. Over time, different styles have been designed with particular spirits and drinks in mind: for example, a brandy snifter is shaped so that the liquor is gently warmed by the hands; a champagne flute is designed to keep the bubbles in the glass; a straight-sided glass helps to hold the separate layers in a pousse-café. Each recipe in this book recommends the type of glass to use for that particular drink together with, where possible, an alternative suggestion. While the type of glass is important, style and size come down to your own personal taste.

a few simple rules

Keep all ingredients cool: chill juices and mixers, champagnes and vermouths. Akavits and vodkas can even be kept in the freezer.

Wash your mixing equipment between making different cocktails to avoid mixing flavours. Rinse spoons and stirrers, too!

Have all of your equipment – tin-opener, bottle-opener, shaker, jigger, mixing glass, bar spoon, straws and stirrers – ready to hand.

Prepare everything but the drink – glasses, fruit juices, fruit garnishes and ingredients like sugar syrup, lemon and lime juices and coconut cream – in advance of your guests arriving.

Always make sure that you have plenty of ice. A well-insulated, large-capacity ice bucket is better than a 'novelty' design, and tongs are more efficient than a spoon (to prevent you ending up with unwanted water).

All glasses must be spotless! After washing, you can avoid stains by polishing glasses completely dry with a clean glass cloth.

A beautiful glass will always give maximum visual impact. There are, naturally, 'classic' glasses for particular drinks, but there are infinite designs to choose from.

Look for glasses with a fine rim and a slender stem (when appropriate), which is long enough that the cool drink is not warmed by the hand's heat.

Choose a glass that suits the drink it will hold – the right size and the right shape, and, if necessary, heat-proof for hot toddies. The recipes in this book advise you which type of glass to use. Useful glasses include the following.

Cocktail glass Elegant and essential, these hold around 120–150ml (4–5 fl oz), with a stem long enough to protect the bowl from the heat of the hand and the opening wide enough to display a garnish where required.

Highball This is a tallish glass, between 230–280g (8–10 oz). It is a useful glass that can serve many different purposes.

Collins glass

Collins This is used for long drinks – the taller the better. Collins glasses, unlike highballs, always have perfectly straight sides. It has around 280–380g (10–12 oz) capacity.

Traditional cocktail

Highball glass

> **Glass-cleaning cloth** You need a glass-cleaning cloth to keep your glassware sparkling and free from the bits of lint that ordinary 'linens' tend to leave behind.

Balloon

Old-fashioned

Champagne flute

Balloon A 'balloon' is basically a red-wine glass, with a 240–300ml (8–10fl oz) capacity. Choose a well-rounded balloon that has plenty of room for ice and garnishes. Coloured drinks look particularly attractive in these glasses. You can also use a large balloon as a goblet, of desired.

Old-fashioned Also called a rocks glass, this is used for any cocktail served 'on the rocks'. It has a 170–230g (6–8 oz) capacity, so is a good size.

Champagne saucer and champagne flute
The traditional champagne saucer was used when dunking Madeira cake in champagne was fashionable. Although elegant and easily recognisable, the open saucer shape lets the bubbles dissipate quickly, allowing the drink to go 'flat'. Nevertheless, some cocktails are traditionally served in a champagne saucer. Champagne flutes are stemmed, narrow, tulip-shaped glasses. Not only do they look pleasing, flutes also retain the bubbles in a drink for longer.

Preparing glasses
Some drinks, like the Margarita, have a frosted effect on the rim of the glass. This is done using either sugar or salt (depending on the drink). SImply dampen the rim of a pre-chilled glass with a slice of lemon (or lime) and dip the rim into a saucer of castor sugar or salt.

Remember to pick the glass up by its stem or by the bottom of the glass to avoid disturbing the frost or marking the glass with fingerprints.

Champagne saucer

hosting tips

Make sure your guests arrive home safely by following these 10 tips when hosting a cocktail party.

1. Avoid drinking too much yourself. As the host or hostess, you can avoid potential problems if you can think clearly and act quickly.

2. Plan your evening in advance so that it's easy to act responsibly. Having a rough schedule in place for eating and pacing the drinking can avoid things getting out of hand.

3. Stop serving alcohol at least an hour before the party is over. Offer alcohol-free drinks and food. Bear in mind that coffee doesn't make a person sober.

4. Find out how guests will be going home after your party. Promote the use of designated drivers and encourage guests to leave thier cars at home and take public transportation, cabs or walk. Have cash and phone numbers ready for taxi companies.

5. Plan to deal with guests who drink too much. Before the party gets rolling, it is a good idea to ask somone reliable to be prepared to help you keep things under control.

6. Mix and serve drinks yourself or designate a bartender instead of having an open bar. Avoid doubles and keep a shot glass or jigger handy to measure drinks. Guests usually drink more when they serve themselves.

7. Be prepared to take away car keys and to have overnight guests. Have blankets and sleeping bags ready.

8. Always serve food with drinks. It is better to eat before or while drinking than to drink on an empty stomach. Offer high-starch and protein foods such as meats, vegetables, cheeses, breads and light dips. Avoid salty, sweet or greasy foods, which will make guests thirsty.

9. Always have low-alcohol and alcohol-free drinks, such as coffee, pop and juice available.

10. Don't plan physical acivities when you serve alcohol. People are more prone to injurt or mishap after drinking.

cocktail terminology

BUILD: Layering the ingredients by pouring directly into the drinking glass.

DASH: A tiny amount, a drop.

GARNISH: Decorate or attach something to the rim of the glass.

LONG: A drink with five measures or more of liquid.

MUDDLE: Mashing or grinding herbs, such as mint, into a smooth paste in the bottom of a glass.

ON THE ROCKS: A drink poured over ice.

SHAKE: 8 to 10 seconds in a cocktail shaker: the whole shaker should feel cold.

SHORT: A drink with less than five measures of liquid before shaking.

STRAIGHT UP: A drink mixed and served without ice.

STRAIN: Pour a drink through a strainer, leaving behind the ice and any other solids.

SHOOTER: A short drink, usually downed 'in one'.

TWIST: 3–6 cm (1–2 inches) length of pith-free citrus peel, held 'skin side' over a drink and twisted in the middle to release the essential oil. The peel is usually discarded but can, if preferred, be dropped in the drink.

Dos and Don'ts

Do get into the habit of adding the cheapest ingredients – such as juices – to the shaker or mixing glass first. If you make a mistake early on, you won't have wasted too much valuable spirit.

Do serve drinks with a mixer in a highball glass. Fill the glass two-thirds full with ice and add the ingredients.

Do use a mixing glass for cocktails containing only alcoholic products.

Do shake sharply for about 8 to 10 seconds when using a shaker.

Do serve cocktails immediately. If you leave them to stand they will separate.

Do wash the shaker or mixing glass after each 'batch'. Sugar/syrup needs attention as it will make the join in the shaker sticky.

Don't shake fizzy drinks!

Don't re-use ice cubes. Always use clean ice.

Don't add alcoholic bitters or syrups to non-alcoholic mocktails.

Don't force an alcoholic drink on anyone.

Don't forget that the volume of a drink will increase when mixed with ice. Make sure your chosen glass is large enough to hold it.

Don't forget the teetotallers and drivers. Do not encourage underage drinking, drink-driving, drunkenness, or anti-social behaviour.

REMEMBER

Cocktails are delicious and easy to drink, but they are often very alcoholic. If you're thirsty, drink water or juice. A cocktail is for sipping and enjoying with friends. Think of American humorist and playwright George Ade's words from his play
The Sultan of Sula (1903):

R-E-M-O-R-S-E!

Those dry Martinis did the work for me;

Last night at twelve I felt immense,

Today I feel like thirty cents.

Vodka Cocktails

Pure vodka is a clear, colourless and smooth spirit with a neutral taste. In Russia, Sweden and Finland it is distilled from a mixture of grains, primarily wheat or barley, and sometimes rye. The Polish distill potatoes to produce Luksusowa and Cracovia vodkas. Beyond the Slav regions, other vodkas are made from a variety of raw materials, which range from beet in Turkey to molasses in Britain.

The world's strongest commercially marketed spirit, vodka was originally produced by the Slavs in a bid to find a very strong spirit that would not freeze in extreme weather (alcohol freezes at a lower temperature than water). Polish Pure Spirit is an immense 80 per cent alcohol by volume (abv), while Spirytus Rektyfikowany ('Rectified Spirit') tops 95 per cent. The more familiar, neutral (unflavoured) vodkas are less strong and include those produced by Smirnoff and that originated in the city of Lvov, once a Polish city, but now in the Ukraine.

Unflavoured vodkas lend themselves perfectly to mixed drinks and are the basis of many a cocktail, such as the sea breeze, the bloody Mary and the screwdriver. Flavoured vodkas have also become very popular in recent years. During the mid-19th century in Poland and Russia, more than a hundred styles of spiced and fruit vodka were available, including the viper vodka, Zmijowka, and the world-famous Zubrowka. No longer sold commercially, Zmijowka involved mascerating a viper snake in vodka for several weeks!

Zubrowka is flavoured with bison grass, a wild herb eaten by European bison roaming the Bialoweiza Forest in eastern Poland. There is a blade of grass in each bottle. Other popular flavours for vodka are cherry, lemon (and lime) and pepper (flavoured with red peppers).

There's an old Russian saying that vodka is only ever drunk for a reason, and that if you happen to have a bottle, you'll find a reason. Every one of the recipes that follows is reason enough!
Really chill your vodka before use: because of its high alcohol content, unflavoured vodka can be placed to chill in the freezer without freezing.

vodka cocktails

black russian

This drink was originally served as a
short drink, either on the rocks or
shaken and strained. During the
1950s, however, cola was added to
make a long drink, and this became
a more popular version.

Ingredients:

2 to 3 ice cubes

$1\frac{1}{2}$ measures vodka

1 measure Tia Maria

cold cola, as required (long
version only)

Method:

Simply place the ingredients in a shaker, shake
well and strain into a cocktail glass.

To build a short version, fill an old-fashioned
glass two-thirds full with ice cubes, pour the
vodka in first, then the Tia Maria, and stir.

To build a long version, fill a highball glass with
ice cubes, pour in the vodka, then the Tia
Maria, and top with cold cola.

Serve with straws.

screwdriver

The screwdriver was not widely known before the 1950s. The name of the drink is thought to come from an American oilman working in Iraq, who apparently stirred his drink with his screwdriver. Another account, given by N E Beveridge in *Cups of Valor*, reports of marines stationed in Teintsin, north-east China, in 1945, who made their own 'screwdriver gin', stirring it with a 46-cm (18-inch) screwdriver.

Ingredients:

ice cubes
4½ measures orange juice
2 measures vodka
1 orange slice
1 maraschino cherry
1 screwdriver (optional)

Method:

Fill a highball glass half-full with ice, pour in the orange juice, then the vodka. Stir – you can use a screwdriver if you like! – and garnish with an orange slice and a maraschino cherry.

Make a 'green eyes' by adding ½ measure of blue Curaçao to a screwdriver. Replace the vodka with white rum, and you have a 'rumscrew'. Use 1 measure of vodka and 1 measure of sloe gin, and you have a 'slow screw', while equal measures of vodka and Wild Turkey result in a 'wild screw'. Add 3 measures of 7-Up to a screwdriver, and you've made yourself a 'screw-up'.

vodka cocktails

bloody mary

The combination of tomato juice and vodka was well known as an apéritif before the 1920s, but it was not until 1921 that the name 'bloody Mary' was first coined, by Fernand 'Pete' Petiot, of Harry's Bar in Paris. Legend has it that the spiced mix was named after Mary Pickford, the famous screen actress of the day. In 1933, Petiot travelled to New York at the invitation of John Astor, of the St Regis Hotel, where he became head barman of the King Cole Grill.

Ingredients:

ice cubes

2 measures vodka

5 measures tomato juice

$1/2$ tsp lemon juice

2 dashes Worcestershire sauce

4 drops Tabasco sauce

1 pinch celery salt

1 pinch black pepper

1 stick celery

Method:

Pour all of the ingredients except the celery into a shaker with some ice cubes, and shake well. Strain into a goblet or large wine glass – over ice, if you wish – and garnish with the celery stick.

Add 1 measure of gold tequila to get a 'deadly Mary'. Use only tequila – and no vodka at all – to make a 'bloody Maria'!

kangaroo & vodkatina

These two vodka cocktails are variations on a martini. They both use the same ingredients and are stirred, not shaken. The only difference between them is the choice of garnish.

Ingredients:

3 to 4 ice cubes

$^3/_4$ measure dry vermouth

$1^1/_2$ measures vodka

I thin strip of lemon peel or
I olive

Method:

Place the ice cubes in a mixing glass and pour in the dry vermouth and vodka. Stir and strain into a chilled cocktail glass.

To make a kangaroo, squeeze a thin strip of lemon peel over the glass to release the oil, then drop the peel into the glass.

For a vodkatini, spear an olive on a cocktail stick and drop into the glass.

silver bullet

Among the ingredients of this classic cocktail is kümmel, a liqueur made with caraway, cumin, fennel, oris and a host of other herbs. Originally made in the late 16th century by Lucas Bols in Amsterdam, kümmel was taken to the distillery at Allasch Castle, near Riga in Latvia by the Russian tsar, Peter the Great. He was working incognito as a labourer in the Dutch shipyards at the time.

Ingredients:

3 to 4 ice cubes

1 measure kümmel

1 $^1/_2$ measures vodka

Method:

Place the ice cubes in a mixing glass and pour in the kümmel and vodka. Stir briefly before straining the liquid into a cocktail glass.

vodka cocktails

cosmopolitan

Ingredients:

ice cubes
1½ measures vodka
1 measure triple sec
or Cointreau
1 dash cranberry juice
(or to taste)
1 lime twist

This is a relatively new cocktail that originated in America. A martini-style aperitif, it is rapidly growing in popularity.

Method:

Half-fill a shaker with ice cubes and pour in the vodka, triple sec and cranberry juice.

Shake the ingredients sharply and strain into well-chilled cocktail glass.

Twist the lime over the drink and discard. Garnish with a wedge of orange, if desired.

golden russian

'Russia' is associated with a number of vodka-based cocktails, inleuding the Soviet and the Moscow mule. Try a golden Russian on a cold, snowy night!

Ingredients:

broken ice
1½ measures vodka
1 measure Galliano
1 teaspoon lime juice
1 lime slice

Method:

Fill a highball glass three-quarters full with broken ice, and pour in the vodka, Galliano and lime juice. Mix gently.

Garnish the glass with the slice of lime.

vodka cocktails

red square

While its name conjurs images of Moscow's Red Square, the 'red' in this drink is provided by grenadine, made from the sweetened juice of pomegranates. The white crème de cacao adds a distinctly chocolaty taste to the mix.

Ingredients:

6 to 8 ice cubes

$^3/_4$ measure vodka

$^3/_4$ measure white crème de cacao

2 tsps lemon juice

1 $^1/_2$ tsp grenadine

1 maraschino cherry

Method:

Half-fill a shaker with ice and add all of the remaining ingredients, except for the cherry.

Strain into a cocktail glass and perch the maraschino cherry on the rim.

moscow mule

Despite its name, the Moscow mule was invented in America by one John Martin, of Heublin & Co. He had acquired the rights to Smirnoff vodka in 1947, and was trying to find ways of encouraging sales. In a chance conversation with Jack Morgan of the Cock 'n' Bull Saloon in Los Angeles, Martin discovered that Morgan was overstocked with ginger ale. By combining the two, with a dash of lime juice, he created the Moscow mule, originally serving it in a copper mug.

Ingredients:

broken ice cubes
2 measures vodka
1 measure lime juice
4 measures ginger ale
1 lime slice
1 orange slice

Method:

Fill a highball or Collins glass almost full with broken ice, and pour in the vodka and lime juice. Add the ginger ale and stir well.

Garnish the glass with lime and orange slices.

vodka cocktails

harvey wallbanger

Rumour has it that the Harvey Wallbanger derives its name from a Californian surfer (called Harvey), who, having lost a major surfing contest, consoled himself with his usual screwdriver, but with added Galliano. Several drinks later, he was seen bumping into furniture and even colliding with a wall. And so a legend was born!

Ingredients:

3 to 4 ice cubes

5 measures orange juice

2 measures vodka

$^3/_4$ measure Galliano

I orange slice

Method:

Place the ice cubes in a highball glass, pour in the orange juice and vodka and sprinkle the Galliano on top. Garnish with an orange slice.

Replace the vodka with gold tequila to make a 'Freddy Fudpucker'.

absolut angel

Ingredients:

3 to 4 ice cubes

$1/2$ measure apple schnaps

1 measure Absolut vodka

$1/2$ tbsp white crème de cacao

1 measure double cream

grated nutmeg

Hailing from the makers of Absolut vodka, this recipe makes use of crème de cacao and apple schnaps. According to Ian Wisniewski, one of the UK's foremost authorities on spirits, Austrian 'schnaps sessions' are often accompanied by a drinking song that includes the line, 'Schnaps was his last word, then the angels took him away'!

Method:

Place the ice cubes in a shaker and pour over the apple schnaps and the Absolut vodka.

Add the crème de cacao and the cream, then shake vigorously.

Strain into a cocktail glass and sprinkle the mix with a little grated nutmeg.

slow, comfortable screw

Almost everyone has heard of this cocktail, but not many know what goes in it! The 'slow' stands for sloe gin, the 'comfortable' represents Southern Comfort and the 'screw' comes from the classic screwdriver: vodka and orange juice.

Ingredients:

3 to 4 ice cubes

1 measure vodka

³/₄ measure Southern Comfort

³/₄ measure sloe gin

5 measures orange juice

1 good scoop broken ice

1 orange slice

Method:

Put the ice cubes in a shaker and pour over the vodka, Southern Comfort, sloe gin and orange juice.

Shake well and strain into a tall highball or Collins glass half-filled with broken ice.

Garnish the glass with an orange slice and sip through a straw.

For a 'slow, comfortable screw against the wall'? sprinkle ¹/₂ measure of Galliano over the top of the cocktail before serving.

vodka cocktails

liberator

This mango-flavored cocktail has a tropical taste to it – perfect for feeling free and easy.

Ingredients:

ice cubes

1 ½ measures vodka

½ measure Midori melon
   liqueur

2 measures mango juice

½ measure lime juice

Method:

Pour all of the ingredients into a shaker with ice cubes and shake well before straining into a cocktail glass.

Garnish with a slice of lime.

vodka silver fizz

'Fizzes' date from the 19th century and are served in tall glasses no more than half-filled with ice, so giving the chilled soda water plenty of room to really fizz and sparkle. It's the addition of egg white that brings this fizz its silver status. The egg is effectively 'cooked' by the vodka, but imparts no taste to the drink. A great, long drink for a summer's day, this is fruity and slightly bitter, making it very refreshing.

Ingredients:

10 to 12 ice cubes

2 measures vodka

1 measure lemon juice

$^3/_4$ measure sugar syrup

1 egg white

chilled soda water, as required

Method:

Half-fill a shaker with ice and pour in all of the remaining ingredients, except for the soda water.

Shake well to froth up the egg white.

Strain into a tall, highball or collins glass half-filled with ice, and top up with chilled soda water.

vodka cocktails

sea breeze

The sea breeze is so popular that it has become a modern classic. Despite its fruitiness, this is quite a 'dry' drink. It's not too sweet and has a lovely colour, thanks to the cranberry juice.

Ingredients:

1 good scoop broken ice

2 measures grapefruit juice

3 measures cranberry juice

1 ½ measures vodka

1 lime wedge

Method:

Place some broken ice in a shaker and pour over the juices and the vodka.

Shake and pour, unstrained, into a highball glass.

Garnish the glass with a lime wedge.

Replace the grapefruit juice with pineapple juice, to make a 'bay breeze'.

Whisky Cocktails

'Whisky' is derived from the Gaelic word *usquebaugh*, which means 'water of life'. Spelled without an 'e' in Scotland and Canada, whiskey (with an 'e') comes from Ireland, the United States and Japan. Single-malt whiskies from Scotland are imbued with the character and flavours unique to their location, imparted to them by the water and the flavour of the germinated barley, which is dried over smoky peat fires, mashed, fermented, distilled and matured in wooden caskets for ten to twelve years. A blended 'Scotch' contains anything from a dozen to forty different malts and two or three grain whiskies. In Ireland, the barley is dried in a kiln rather than over a peat fire, which brings forth an entirely different flavour altogether.

Like Scotland, each of the whiskey-producing states in the US has its own style. Scottish immigrants made rye whiskey in Pennsylvania and Maryland before moving to Kentucky, a state better suited to growing Indian corn (maize), and distilling began in earnest during the late 1700s. The famous blue-grass whiskey comes from Kentucky, which lies on a massive limestone shelf, where the water is hard. . At least 51 per cent of bourbon whiskey mash must be maize, the rest being rye (for flavour) and malted barley (for fermentability). The particular vanilla and softly fruited flavours in bourbon owe much to the use of new, charred, oak barrels for ageing, which takes from six to eight years. The barrels can only be used once, after which they are used by the distillers of Caribbean rum and Scotch! Like Scotch, bourbon is available either blended or 'straight', which means that it has been distilled from a single grain and that all of the whiskey comes from a single distiller. A well-known brand of straight Kentucky bourbon is Wild Turkey.

Historically, rye was the first whiskey produced in the United States, and has a spicy, even minty, flavour because of the use of a minimum of 51 per cent rye grains (the rest being maize and barley). It is matured for about four years in new, charred, oak barrels.

Tennessee whiskey must, by law, be produced in the state of Tennessee. It is filtered through wood charcoal, which results in a very mild flavour. Some of the best-known brands – like Jack Daniels, from Lynchburg, which is filtered through maple chippings – are distinct from bourbon because they are produced from a sour mash that contains previously fermented yeast. Fresh yeast makes a sweet mash, while, in Tennessee, the already fermented yeast (similar to that used to make sourdough bread) makes for a sour mash.

highball

Ingredients:

ice cubes

$\frac{1}{2}$ measure bourbon

5 measures soda (or ginger ale)

This drink was so popular in the US during the first quarter of the 20th century, that *The New York Times* set out to discover the truth about its origins. Investigations revealed that New York barman, Patrick Duffy, created the highball, in around 1895. The drink took its name from the 19th-century American railroad practice of raising a ball on a high pole as a signal to train drivers to increase their speed. Since a 'highball' meant 'hurry', Duffy's drink was one that could be made quickly, simply by pouring the ingredients over ice in a tall glass.

Method:

Drop 3 or 4 ice cubes into a highball glass, pour in the bourbon and top with soda or ginger ale.

Add a lemon twist (optional), and stir lightly.

marimba

Just like the musical instrument from which this cocktail takes its name, this tropical-fruit-flavored cocktail is certain to get you dancing.

Ingredients:

1 measure Southern Comfort

$^1\!/_2$ measure gin

$^1\!/_4$ measure amaretto

1 measure pineapple juice

1 measure mango juice

$^1\!/_4$ measure lime juice

Method:

Place all of the ingredients in a shaker with some ice cubes and shake rhythmically for 10 seconds.

Strain into a cocktail glass and garnish with pineapple and orange slices, if desired.

whisky cocktails

mint julep

This bourbon refresher is traditionally served on Kentucky Derby Day – the first Saturday in May, and no other tall drink is so delicious. Such is its fame that there is much debate as to how it should be made.

Should the mint be crushed? Should it be left in the glass or taken out? Should you drink a mint julep through a straw? An early record of this drink was written by an English teacher, John Davis, in 1803, while he was working in Virginia. He described the julep as a 'dram of spirituous liquor that has mint in it' and also noted that the Virginians drank it in the mornings as an 'eye-opener'. The 'spirituous liquor' Davis mentioned was most likely brandy. After the Civil War, bourbon became more widely available and has long been the most popular base spirit for the cocktail.

Ingredients:

1 measure gomme syrup
4 sprigs mint – use small, tender leaves, and add more if you like it!
3 measures bourbon – Kentucky bourbon is best
crushed ice – as fine as possible (the more like snow the better!)
mint sprigs

Method:

Pour the gomme syrup into a pre-chilled Collins glass and add the sprigs of mint.

Gently crush the mint with a muddler. This is an optional instruction – some refuse to crush the mint at all.

Add the bourbon and stir gently while filling the glass with crushed ice.

Clip off the end of each mint sprig so that the juice flows into the julep and arrange the sprigs of mint on top of the drink. Serve with straws and a stirrer.

cranberry cooler

Ingredients:

1½ measures bourbon

1½ measures cranberry juice

½ measure lime juice

1 teaspoon sugar

Kentucky Derby Day isn't the only time to enjoy bourbon. National Bourbon Week takes place in September, so why not celebrate with a few favourites!

Method:

Combine all the ingredients in a blender with a glass of crushed ice and blend until smooth.

Pour the drink into a parfait or white wine glass to serve.

old-fashioned

This classic whiskey cocktail can be made with any American whiskey, although some insist on using rye. It first appeared at the Pendennis Club in Louisville, Kentucky, in 1900, where it was made especially at the request of bourbon distiller, Colonel James E Pepper. It is a simple affair that involves adding bourbon to a glass containing a bitters-soaked sugar cube that has been topped up with ice.

Ingredients:

broken ice

2 measures bourbon

1 sugar cube

1 dash bitters

1 dash soda water (optional)

Method:

Place the sugar cube in an old-fashioned glass and add the dash of bitters. When the sugar has soaked up all of the bitters, fill the glass three-quarters full with broken ice.

Pour in the whiskey, and add the garnish and dash of soda water (optional). Serve with a muddler.

whisky cocktails

new york

This cocktail makes for a fitting

toast to the Big Apple!

Ingredients:

ice cubes

broken ice

³⁄₄ measure lime juice

¹⁄₂ measure gomme syrup

1 teaspoon grenadine

2 measures whisky – traditionally, Canadian whisky

Method:

Half-fill a shaker with ice cubes, and pour in the lime juice, gomme syrup, grenadine and whisky.

Shake well and strain immediately into an old-fashioned glass three-quarters filled with broken ice.

Add a twist of orange to garnish, if desired.

morning-glory fizz

First mentioned during the 1870s, a fizz is traditionally served in the morning, or at midday at the latest. A fizz is made by shaking the ingredients before adding soda, or alternative sparkling mixer.

Ingredients:

1 tsp caster sugar

1 $^1/_3$ measures lemon juice

6 to 8 ice cubes

1 dash angostura bitters

2 measures Scotch whisky

$^1/_4$ measure egg white

4 measures soda water

1 orange slice

Method:

First dissolve the caster sugar in the lemon juice. Then place half of the ice cubes in a shaker and pour in the juice, bitters, Scotch and egg white.

Shake well and strain the liquid into a Collins glass half-filled with the remaining ice.

Top with the soda water and garnish the glass with a slice of orange. Serve with a muddler.

whisky cocktails

rhett butler

Ingredients:

crushed ice

2 measures Southern Comfort

¼ measure triple sec/Cointreau

¼ measure lime juice

¼ measure lemon juice

What would Scarlet O'Hara be without Rhett Butler? And don't say that you frankly don't give a damn!

Method:

Place a good scoopful of crushed ice into a shaker and pour in the Southern Comfort, triple sec, lemon and lime juices.

Shake well and pour, unstrained, into an old-fashioned glass. Garnish with a lemon peel twist, if desired, and serve with a short straw.

scarlett o'hara

Southern Comfort is the obvious choice for this pretty pink belle. Its peachy flavor makes for terrific frozen sour-type drinks.

Ingredients:

crushed ice

2 measures Southern Comfort

1 measure grenadine

1 dash lime juice

Method:

Place a good scoopful of crushed ice into a shaker and pour in the Southern Comfort, grenadine and lime juice.

Shake well and pour, unstrained, into a cocktail or champagne saucer. Serve with short straws.

whisky cocktails

manhattan

The Manhattan is one of the all time classic cocktails, and is reputed to have been invented in around 1874 at the Manhattan Club in New York for Winston Churchill's mother, Lady Randolph Churchill. Originally, the drink was made with one measure whiskey and two measures vermouth and served straight up. Today, it is more often served on the rocks and with a lot less vermouth. Rye whiskey was the traditional choice, but many prefer bourbon these days.

Ingredients:

broken ice

2 measures rye or bourbon

1 measure rosso vermouth

1 dash bitters

1 maraschino cherry

Method:

Place a glass full of broken ice into the shaker, then pour in the whiskey, vermouth and bitters.

Shake briefly and pour unstrained into an old-fashioned glass.

Garnish with the cherry.

thunderclap

Ingredients:

ice cubes

1½ measures whisky of choice

1 measure gin

1 measure brandy

Too many of these, and that's what a dropping pin will sound like the morning after!

Method:

Half-fill a mixing glass with ice cubes, the pour in the whisky, gin and brandy.

Stir well and strain into a cocktail glass.

Irish Blackthorn

The fruit of the blackthorn are the sloes used in making sloe gin, while its wood is traditionally used to make shillelaghs (clubs or cudgels). This cocktail should use Irish whiskey for authenticity. In Ireland, the barley is dried in a kiln rather than over a peat fire, which is the method tradtionally used for Scotch whisky.

Ingredients:

6 to 8 ice cubes

1 $\frac{1}{2}$ measures Irish whiskey

1 $\frac{1}{2}$ measures dry vermouth

3 dashes Pernod

3 dashes angostura bitters

Method:

Place half of the ice cubes in a mixing glass and pour in the remaining ingredients.

Strain the liquid into a rocks glass filled with the remaining ice.

whisky cocktails

the sour

Ingredients:

ice cubes

1 measure lemon juice

1/2 measure gomme syrup

2 measures whisky

The first sours, made in the 1850s, were brandy sours. Since that time, however, the drink has been made with almost every base spirit available and the whisky sour is now one of the most popular versions. Its name derives from the fact that very little sweetener and a relatively large amount of lemon juice is used. It is usually drunk from a stemmed sour glass, but can also be served in an old-fashioned glass topped up with soda water. While a sour should never taste sweet, you can adjust the amount of sugar to suit your taste. You can also have gin sour, a vodka sour, a tequila sour, a rum sour and a brandy sour.

Method:

Half-fill a shaker with ice cubes and pour in the lemon juice and gomme syrup.

Add the whisky, shake well and strain into a sour glass.

If you prefer your sours with a dash of soda water, serve on the rocks in an old-fashioned glass.

waldorf cocktail

This is a classic cocktail, created in honour of one of the finest hotels in New York, which also happens to be one of the city's great architectural masterpieces. Bourbon is usually the whiskey of choice, but you can subtly alter the end result by trying different blends.

Ingredients:

1 good scoop crushed ice

1 dash angostura bitters

1 measure sweet vermouth

1 measure Pernod

2 measures bourbon

Method:

Place a good scoop of crushed ice in a mixing glass and pour in the angostura bitters, sweet vermouth, Pernod and bourbon.

Stir well and strain the liquid into a pre-chilled cocktail glass.

whisky cocktails

fly swatter

Ingredients:

broken ice

1 measure cognac

1 measure whiskey

1 teaspoon Pernod or Ricard

3 measures mandarin juice

2 measures pineapple juice

The original recipe for the fly swatter calls for raki, the aniseed-tinged aperitif of Greece and Turkey. Pernod or Ricard, make just as good a version, however.

Method:

Add the ingredients to an oversized wine glass or goblet filled with broken ice.

Top with a sprig of mint and serve with straws.

gin cocktails

Gin is often thought to be quintessentially English but, in fact, it originally developed in Holland as a rye spirit flavoured with juniper . It was introduced to the English during the 16th century when, in 1585, English mercenaries were sent to the Low Countries to aid the Dutch in their fight against the Spanish overlord, King Philip II. When the soldiers returned to England, they brought gin with them, where it was distilled as 'geneva'.

William of Orange became king of Great Britain and Ireland in 1689, further strengthening theDutch influence in England at the time. When Britain went to war with France during the early 18th century, William raised the import duty on brandy and gave everyone in England the right to distil spirits. Gin thus began to develop its English identity.

Gin is, basically, a neutral, grain spirit that is distilled a second time with 'botanicals': a range of herbs, spices and fruits that might include juniper, coriander, angelica, ginger, nutmeg, lemon and orange peel, almonds, cassia bark, cinnamon and liquorice root. The alcoholic strength of the gin influences the flavour imparted by the botanicals: the stronger the gin, the more intense their flavour. Plymouth gin, made with water from Devon (also the gin favoured for pink gin), is available at a hefty 57 per cent alcohol by volume (abv). London gin is a particular style of dry gin at 37.5 per cent abv. What is known as sloe gin is not a true gin, but rather a liqueur, made by macerating sloes – the small, dark fruit of the blackthorn – in gin.

A Spanish gin, Larios, has been made since 1863, and in the Netherlands, there are three main styles of 'genever' based on wheat, rye, maize and malted barley: young genever, old genever and korenwijn. The difference between young and old genevers is not their age, but the difference in recipes: old genever follows the traditional recipe, and is a slightly sweeter, more aromatic, straw-coloured spirit than the clear, young genever. Korenwijn is made of the finest-quality grain distillates, which are then aged in oak barrels. Bols' korenwijn is matured for three years before being bottled in the famous, handmade, 'stone' jars.

Gin is among the most common base spirits for cocktails, and central to the most famous cocktail of all, the martini. America's Prohinition era was a time of great cocktail invention, largely because the only gin available was bathtub gin. Concocted illegally in a bathtub, this bootleg gin bore little, if any, relation to the premium gins available outside of America, and would have been pretty unpleasant drunk neat. Bartenders therefore disguised its rawness with bitters, juices and other spirits and liqueurs, finding it to be a most versatile spirit.

harry's cocktail

Ingredients:

ice cubes

²/₃ measure gin

¹/₃ measure sweet vermouth

1 dash absinthe (substitute: Pernod or Ricard)

2 sprigs of mint

This cocktail is named after the great Harry MacElhone of the Casino Bar, Aix-les-Bains, France, who created the drink in 1910.

Method:

Shake all the ingredients in a shaker with some ice cubes.

Strain into a chilled cocktail glass and serve with a stuffed olive.

lemon flip

The flip takes its name from the method of flipping them to and fro between two vessels in order to obtain a smooth mix. Flips first became popular during the 1690s, when they were made of beaten eggs, sugar, spices, rum and hot ale. They still contain egg yolk today, but are served short and cold. This shouldn't put you off: the egg is effectively 'cooked' by the alcohol.

Ingredients:

3 to 4 ice cubes

1$^1/_2$ measures lemon juice

1 measure gin

$^3/_4$ measure Cointreau

1 yolk of a small egg

$^1/_2$ lemon slice

Method:

Place the ice in a shaker and add all of the remaining ingredients except for the $^1/_2$ slice of lemon.

Shake firmly, strain the liquid into a champagne flute and garnish the glass with the lemon.

gin cocktails

martini

Ingredients:

Dry martini

6 to 8 ice cubes

1 measure gin

1 measure dry vermouth

1 green olive

Medium martini

6 to 8 ice cubes

1 measure gin

1 measure dry vermouth

1 measure sweet vermouth

Sweet martini

6 to 8 ice cubes

1 measure gin

1 measure sweet vermouth

1 cocktail cherry

There are as many variations of the martini as there are bartenders in the world! Each has his or her own favourite recipe but, in general, the difference lies in the degree of sweetness imparted by the vermouth, and the garnish used. The following recipes are all made using the same method – stirred and not shaken – and range from dry through medium to sweet. The picture shows a dry martini.

Method:

Place the ice cubes in a mixing glass and pour in the gin and vermouth.

Stir – some say 12 times, others say 20 – it is up to you.

Strain the liquid into a well-chilled cocktail glass and garnish appropriately.

gimlet

Ingredients:

ice cubes

2 measures gin (some insist on Plymouth gin)

¾ measure lime cordial

1 measure cold soda water (optional)

A gimlet is a small, pointed hand tool used for boring holes in wood. Often used in bars to tap into barrels, the gimlet soon lent its name to a short, sharp cocktail. The drink seems originally to have been concocted by British residents in the Far East after the First World War. gin and lime juice are the two ingredients. Some say that freshly squeezed lime juice was used, while others maintain that lime cordial, which is concentrated and sweetened, was preferred. Although limes were probably plentiful, the British may well have used the cordial since it predates the gimlet recipes.

Method:

Fill an old-fashioned glass with ice and pour in the gin and lime cordial.

Stir, add soda if desired and garnish with the wedge of lime.

suzy wong

This fruity, yet dry, cocktail makes use of both gin and Mandarine Napoleon, a form of Curaçao made in Belgium by macerating tangerines in aged cognac. The cocktail is named after actress Suzi Wong, whom Emperor Napoleon is said to have wooed.

Ingredients:

1 lemon wedge

caster sugar

6 to 8 ice cubes

$^3/_4$ measure lemon juice

$^3/_4$ measure gin

$^3/_4$ measure Mandarine Napoleon

chilled champagne or sparkling white wine, to top up

orange peel

Method:

Run the wedge of lemon around the rim of a champagne saucer to wet it, and dip the glass into the caster sugar.

Place plenty of ice in a shaker and add all of the remaining ingredients except for the champagne and orange garnish.

Shake well and strain the liquid into a champagne saucer.

Top with chilled champagne and garnish the glass with the orange peel.

gin cocktails

alexander's sister

Ingredients:

3 to 4 ice cubes

$3/4$ measure gin

$3/4$ measure green crème de menthe

$3/4$ measure double cream

The traditional Alexander is made with brandy, while his little sister is a gin-based, creamy and minty affair. The mint flavour and the pale, eau-de-nil colour come from the green crème de menthe, a sweet liqueur distilled from various types of mint.

Method:

Place the ice in a shaker and add all of the remaining ingredients.

Shake well and strain the liquid into a pre-chilled cocktail glass.

caesar ritz

This subtle, fruit-flavored cocktail was created at the Hotel Ritz in Paris. It uses a touch of Kirsch – a colorless 'eau de vie' distilled from whole black cherries and their stones.

Ingredients:

ice cubes

2 measures gin

²/₃ measure dry vermouth

¹/₃ measure cherry brandy

¹/₃ measure Kirsch

red cherry

Method:

Pour all the ingredients into a mixing glass with some ice cubes and stir well.

Strain the liquid into a pre-chilled cocktail glass and garnish with a Kirsch- soaked red cherry on a cocktail stick.

gin cocktails

Singapore Sling
the original

Ingredients:
3 to 4 ice cubes
1 measure gin
1 measure cherry brandy
$^1/_2$ measure Cointreau
1 measure lime juice
1 measure pineapple juice
1 measure orange juice
$^1/_4$ measure grenadine
1 dash angostura bitters
1 tsp Benedictine
1 pineapple slice
1 maraschino cherry

World-famous, the Singapore sling was created by Ngiam Tong Boon at the Raffles Hotel, in Singapore, in 1915. Originally intended as a lady's drink, it soon became widely enjoyed by both sexes, with writers Somerset Maugham and Joseph Conrad, and the Hollywood actor Douglas Fairbanks claiming it to be a favourite. Some modern versions call for soda water to finish the drink, but in this, the Raffles Hotel Bar version, soda is never used.

Method:

Place the ice cubes in a shaker and pour in all of the remaining ingredients except for the Benedictine and fruit garnishes.

Shake well and strain the liquid into a highball glass three-quarters filled with broken ice. Sprinkle the Benedictine on top.

Garnish with the slice of pineapple and the maraschino cherry and serve with straws.

tom collins

This drink is also known as a John Collins, since the original Collins was called John. (He was head waiter at Limmers Hotel in London during the 18th century). Traditionally, the recipe used a heavy, Dutch-style gin, but this was not popular in America. Instead, a London gin called Old Tom proved more successful, and so the cocktail's name stuck.

Ingredients:

ice cubes

1 measure London dry gin

1 dash sugar syrup

juice of 1 lemon

chilled soda water

1 lemon slice

Method:

Half-fill a highball or Collins glass with ice cubes and pour over the gin, sugar syrup and lemon juice. Stir gently, top up with chilled soda water and garnish the glass with the lemon slice.

A Collins can be made with any spirit: cognac for a Pierre Collins; Irish whiskey for a Mike Collins; Calvados or applejack for a Jack Collins; rum for a Pedro Collins; and tequila for a Juan Collins!

blue lady

The original 'lady' was white, and was made by mixing crème de menthe with Cointreau or Curaçao. In 1929, bartender Harry MacElhone replaced the mint with gin, creating a very popular cocktail in the process. This version uses blue Curaçao, which is still orange flavoured. Feel free to adjust the amount of lemon juice if you prefer a sweeter mix.

Ingredients:

1 lemon wedge

caster sugar

3 to 4 ice cubes

1 measure lemon juice

1 measure gin

1 measure blue Curaçao

1 maraschino cherry

Method:

Run the lemon wedge around the rim of a pre-chilled cocktail glass and dip the glass into the caster sugar to coat it.

Place the ice cubes in a shaker and pour on the lemon juice, gin and blue Curaçao.

Shake well, strain into the cocktail glass, and garnish with a maraschino cherry.

gin cocktails

gin daisy

The 'daisy' is an American invention that has been around since the 1850s. Originally served straight up in a tankard, an old-fashioned glass is more usual today, filled with plenty of broken or crushed ice. A small quantity of fruit syrup is always used and a little seasonal fruit makes for an appropriate garnish. If adding soda, use no more than half the quantity of the spirit.

ice cubes

2 measures gin

1 measure lemon juice

1/2 level teaspoon caster sugar

1 teaspoon grenadine

broken ice

1 measure soda water (optional)

1 maraschino cherry

1 lemon slice

Method:

Half-fill a shaker with ice cubes and add the gin, lemon juice, sugar and grenadine.

Shake well and strain the liquid into an old-fashioned glass filled with broken ice.

Top up with soda if desired, and garnish with a cherry and lemon slice.

delmonico cocktail

This classy cocktail is perfect for sipping on a relaxing evening.

Ingredients:

ice cubes

1 measure gin

1/2 measure brandy

1/2 measure sweet vermouth

1/2 measure dry vermouth

1 dash angostura bitters

Method:

Half-fill a mixing glass with ice cubes and pour in the gin, brandy, vermouths and bitters.

Stir well and strain the liquid into a pre-chilled cocktail glass.

gin cocktails

pink pussycat

Ingredients:

ice cubes

2 measures gin

2–3 measures pineapple juice

2 measures grapefruit juice

$\frac{1}{3}$ measure grenadine

I grapefruit slice

I red cherry

The 'pink' in many a cocktail comes from grenadine: a pink elephant, a pink squirrel and the pink panther.
A pink pussycat uses grapefruit juice and you can adjust the measure to suit your own taste, depending on how sharp you like your pussycat's claws!

Method:

Half-fill the shaker with ice cubes, and pour in the gin, pineapple and grapefruit juices and the grenadine.

Shake well and strain the liquid into an ice-filled Collins glass.

Garnish with a slice of grapefruit (be brave!) and a cherry.

long island iced tea

This drink could be included in many sections of this book, as it contains equal measures of vodka, gin, rum, tequila and triple sec. Early versions were made without the tequila and triple sec.

Ingredients:

ice cubes

broken ice

1/2 measure vodka

1/2 measure gin

1/2 measure tequila

1/2 measure white rum

1/2 measure triple sec or Cointreau

1 measure lemon juice

1/2 measure gomme syrup

3–4 measures cold cola

1 lemon wedge

Method:

Half-fill a shaker with ice cubes, and add the vodka, gin, rum, tequila, rum, triple sec, lemon juice and gomme syrup.

Shake well and strain into a Collins glass half-full with broken ice.

Pour in the cold cola and finish by adding the lemon wedge to the glass.

gin cocktails

royal fizz

The first fizzes were created around the 1890s. Similar to a Collins, they are always shaken before adding the soda water and only use half a glass of ice to ensure that the soda effervesces. Fizzes were traditionally served in the morning or at midday as a pick-me-up.

Ingredients:

6 to 8 ice cubes

$1^{1}/_{2}$ measures gin

$^{3}/_{4}$ measure lemon juice

2 tsps sugar syrup

1 egg

chilled soda water

Method:

Place half of the ice cubes in a shaker and add all of the remaining ingredients except for the soda water. Shake vigourously.

Strain and pour the liquid into a highball or Collins glass half-filled with the remaining ice cubes and top up with soda water.

Make a silver fizz by using just the egg white and not the whole egg.

captain's table

Ingredients:

ice cubes

2 measures gin

½ measure Campari

1 teaspoon grenadine

1 measure orange juice

4 measures ginger ale

1 maraschino cherry

This cocktail includes the bright red, bitter Campari, Italy's most famous aperitif.

Method:

Half-fill a shaker with ice cubes and pour in the gin, Campari, grenadine and orange juice.

Shake well and strain the liquid into a highball glass almost filled with ice cubes.

Top up with the ginger ale and drop a cherry into the glass.

Rum Cocktails

Rum is, famously, the drink of pirates and, until recently, was officially part of British Royal Navy rations. It was also the most commonly traded contraband for centuries. No one knows exactly how rum got its name, although there are several theories. Some say that the name comes from an English West Country dialect, others say that it derives from *saccharum*, the Latin for 'sugar'. The home of rum (or ron or rhum, depending on the drink's ethnicity) is in the Caribbean – Jamaica, Martinique, Puerto Rico, Cuba, the Virgin Islands – and a number of coastal countries in Central and South America. Christopher Columbus introduced sugar to the Caribbean and, with almost every European nation vying for control of the West Indies, each colonial power had its own procedures for producing the spirit. Differing climates and soils also played a part in producing different versions.

There are two ways of making rum: it can be distilled directly from the fermented juice of crushed sugar cane; or the sugar itself can be extracted first, and the rum made from the molasses that remain. A further variation requires the addition of a dunder – the residue from a previous distillation – to make a more potent spirit. Variations in raw materials and the duration of the fermentation process affect the final flavour of the rum.

There are two main methods of distilling rum: one uses pot stills and the other a continuous still. The former has a pear-shaped pot, usually made of copper, in which the materials to be distilled are heated, and a 'swan's neck', which carries the vapour to the condenser. Each distillation is a separate process, after which the still has to be stopped and recharged. If it continued, it would produce a much purer distillate, which would have less flavour. A continuous still, on the other hand, is very efficient at producing purer distillates and light rums (as well as neutral spirits like vodka and gin).

Pot stills are used in the French-speaking countries of the Caribbean to distil cane juice, while in the English-speaking countries, Jamaica produces full-bodied rums from molasses and dunder. Guyana produces its own, unique style of rum known as demerara, which is a dark, but medium-bodied, rum made with molasses in continuous stills. Barbados rum, made in both types of still, is soft and smoky, while Trinidad makes a fine rum in continuous stills. The Spanish-speaking countries use continuous stills to produce a light-bodied rum from molasses.

All rum is clear and colourless, but for light rum to remain clear, it is first matured in pale, ash-wood barrels for a year before being transferred to stainless-steel tanks for ageing. Dark rum is left to mature for five to seven years in dark, wooden casks, where it develops its golden or brown colour and a full-bodied flavour. Light or white rums have a more delicate taste than dark rums, and therefore make for better blends with fruit juices and liqueurs without losing flavour.

piña colada

Ingredients:

I scoop crushed ice

3 measures white rum

4 measures crushed pineapple or pineapple juice

2 measures coconut cream

I tsp sugar syrup (optional)

I pineapple slice

I cherry

The piña colada is one of the true cocktail greats and comes from Puerto Rico. The originator of the drink is disputed: some credit Ramon Marrero Perez, of the Carib Hilton, in 1954, while others say that it was the creation of Don Ramon Portas Mingot, of La Barrachina Restaurant Bar, in 1963. Served properly, it should be drunk from a poco glass, but any large, attractive glass will work just as well.

Method:

Place all of the ingredients except for the sugar syrup and garnishes in a shaker or blender and combine.

Check the drink for sweetness, adding a little sugar syrup if needed.

Strain the liquid into a poco glass and garnish with the fruit.

cuba libre

Legend has it that, an army officer in Havana, Cuba, invented this drink by mixing Bacardi white rum with the newly arrived soft drink Coca Cola. Ask a barman for a 'Bacardi and coke' and you will be served exactly with those two registered brands. Ask for a Cuba libre, however, and he will ask you which light rum you'd prefer!

Ingredients:

$\frac{1}{2}$ lime

ice cubes

2 measures white rum

4–5 measures cold cola

Method:

Squeeze the juice of the $\frac{1}{2}$ lime into a highball glass and drop the spent shell of the lime into the glass.

Fill the glass two-thirds full with ice cubes, pour in the rum and top with cold cola.

Serve the drink with a straw.

rum cocktails

blue hawaiian

Ingredients:

1 glass crushed ice

1 $^1/_2$ measures white rum

$^1/_2$ measure dark rum

$^1/_2$ measure blue Curaçao

3 measures pineapple juice

1 measure coconut cream

1 slice pineapple, to garnish

maraschino cherry

pineapple chunks

Rum, pineapple and coconut feature in this totally tropical mix, with the dark, Jamaican-style rum adding extra fullness. This delicious cocktail was created by Paulo Loureiro, of Claridge's Bar in London's Mayfair.

Method:

Place a glassful of crushed ice in a blender and add all of the remaining ingredients, except from the fruit garnishes.

Blend briefly and pour the liquid into a pre-chilled goblet.

Garnish the glass with the fruit and pop in a short straw.

sun city

This cocktail has a great fruity flavor and is the perfect refreshment for an afternoon in the summer sun.

Ingredients:

ice cubes

1 measure light rum

$\frac{1}{2}$ measure dark rum

$\frac{1}{2}$ measure Galliano

$\frac{1}{2}$ measure apricot brandy

2 measures pineapple juice

juice of $\frac{1}{4}$ lime

4 measures lemonade

Method:

Place all the ingredients except the lemonade into a shaker with two or three ice cubes.

Shake well and strain the liquid into an ice-filled piña colada glass.

Drop in the spent shell of the lime and top up the glass with lemonade.

Serve with straws.

rum cocktails

daiquiri & frozen daiquiri

The original daiquiri, made from rum, lime and sugar, was created in Cuba in 1896 by the American mining engineer Jennings Cox. Its name was taken from the nearby town of Daiquiri at the suggestion of a colleague. The frozen daiquiri was created by Constante Ribailagua of La Floridita Bar in Havana, who worked there from 1912 until his death in 1952. Served with crushed ice, the lime is traditionally squeezed into the mixture by hand in order to release its zesty flavour and aroma.

Ingredients:

$^2/_3$ measure lime juice

2 measures white rum

1 tsp caster sugar

1 lime slice

1 glassful crushed ice (frozen daiquiri only)

Method:

To make an original daiquiri, shake and strain the lime juice, rum and sugar into a chilled champagne saucer, garnish with the lime slice and serve.

For a frozen daiquiri (pictured), place a glassful of crushed ice in a blender and squeeze in the juice of the lime by hand.

Pour in the rum and sugar and blend briefly.

Pour the liquid into a chilled champagne saucer and garnish with a lime slice.

Variations: add $^1/_4$ measure of grenadine for a pink daiquiri, or add $^1/_4$ measure of crème de cassis for a French daiquiri, the creation of Ernest Luthi, of the Stork Club in York, England, in around 1935.

love in the afternoon

Ingredients:

2 measures dark rum

1/2 measure crème de fraise

1 measure orange juice

3/4 measure coconut cream

1/2 measure sugar syrup

1/2 measure whipping cream

4 to 5 strawberries

This is the cocktail for strawberry lovers – and you don't just have to reserve it for afternoons!

Method:

Set aside the best strawberry for the garnish and place the other ingredients in a blender. Blend until smooth.

Add half a glass of crushed ice and blend briefly once more.

Pour the liquid into a piña colada glass, goblet, or hurricane glass and garnish with the strawberry.

monkey wrench

This is a long, refreshing drink that really does justice to grapefruit juice. The lemonade cuts the sharpness a little, and the cherry helps too!

Ingredients:

ice cubes

1¾ measures white rum

3 measures grapefruit juice

3 measures lemonade

1 grapefruit slice

1 maraschino cherry

Method:

Fill a Collins glass two-thirds full with ice cubes.

Pour on the rum and grapefruit juice and top with lemonade.

Garnish the drink with the grapefruit slice and cherry and add straws.

rum cocktails

el presidente

Ingredients:

ice cubes

1 teaspoon grenadine

1/3 measure dry vermouth

1 measure rosso vermouth

2 measures white rum

crushed ice

1 orange slice

1 cherry

There may well be as many variations of the Presidente cocktail as there have been Latin American presidents. While many are simply called 'El Presidente', others are named after a specific president. This recipe is for an El Presidente created in around 1920 at the Vista Alegre Bar in Havana, Cuba, for President General Mario Menocal.

Method:

Half-fill a shaker with ice cubes and pour in the grenadine, dry vermouth, rosso vermouth and white rum.

Shake well and strain the liquid into an old-fashioned glass almost filled with crushed ice.

Garnish with the orange slice and cherry.

bacardi cocktail

Bacardi y Cia, the proprietors of the Bacardi trademark, objected to the name 'Bacardi' being applied to any drink and not just those made with Bacardi rum. In 1937, a New York Supreme Court Ruling found in the firm's favour and Bacardi y Cie now have exclusive rights to the use of the name.

Ingredients:

ice cubes

1 measure lime juice

1 teaspoon grenadine

½ measure gomme syrup

1½ measures Bacardi white rum

1 cherry on a stick

Method:

Half-fill a shaker with ice cubes and pour in the lime juice, grenadine, gomme syrup and Bacardi rum.

Shake well and strain the liquid into a champagne saucer or cocktail glass and garnish with a cherry on a stick.

rum cocktails

frozen miami

Roll up your jacket sleeves and take off your socks for a little taste of Miami Vice in the comfort of your own home!

Ingredients:

crushed ice

2$\frac{1}{2}$ measures light rum

$\frac{1}{2}$ measure white crème de menthe

$\frac{1}{2}$ measure lime juice

Method:

Place a good scoop of crushed ice in a shaker and pour in the rum, crème de menthe and lime juice.

Shake briskly before pouring, unstrained, into a pre-chilled cocktail glass.

Garnish the drink with a sprig of mint and serve with short straws.

zombie

This infamous drink was invented in 1934 by Don Beach at Don the Beachcomber Restaurant in Hollywood, California. Legend has it that Don first made the drink for a guest who was suffering from a hangover and said he felt like a zombie. Don Beach created a total of 63 exotic cocktail recipes and it seems his aim with all of them was to get as much alcohol as possible in a glass! If you don't feel like a zombie before, you may well need one after!

Ingredients:

crushed ice

1/2 measure light rum

1 measure golden rum

1/2 measure dark rum

1/2 measure cherry brandy

1/2 measure apricot brandy

2 measures pineapple juice

1 measure orange juice

3/4 measure lime juice

1/2 measure papaya juice

1/4 measure orgeat

1/3 measure dark rum

Method:

Fill a shaker with a glassful of crushed ice and pour in all the ingredients except the overproof dark rum.

Shake briefly and strain the liquid into a highball glass filled with crushed ice.

Dribble the overproof dark rum on top using a long-handled bar spoon.

Garnish the drink with a sprig of mint and slices of lime and pineapple, if desired.

rum cocktails

mojito

The mojito might also be described as a Cuban mint julep, with its crushed mint leaves at the bottom of the glass. This drink was especially popular during the US Prohibition era, at the Bodeguita del Medico Bar in Havana, Cuba.

Ingredients:

3 to 4 mint sprigs

1 spent lime shell

1 glass crushed or broken ice

2½ measures white rum

juice of ½ lime

1 dash angostura bitters

⅔ measure sugar syrup

3 to 4 ice cubes

2 measures chilled soda water

Method:

Drop the mint sprigs into the bottom of a Collins glass and crush them gently.

Add the spent lime shell and fill the glass with crushed or broken ice.

Place some ice cubes in a shaker and pour in the rum, lime juice, angostura bitters and sugar syrup. Shake gently.

Strain the liquid into the glass and add the soda water.

Top with a little more crushed ice if desired, and then gently muddle the mix together.

Serve with a straw.

maragato special

Emilio Maragato Gonzalez of the Florida Hotel Bar in Cuba created this drink in 1920. At the time the recipe was a closely guarded family secret and remained so until Emilio's death in 1935.

Ingredients:

2 to 3 scoops crushed ice

1 measure white rum

$3/4$ measure dry vermouth

$3/4$ measure red vermouth

$1/2$ tsp maraschino

juice of $1/3$ orange

juice of $1/2$ lime

1 lime slice

Method:

Fill a large cocktail glass with crushed ice.

Place the remaining ice in a shaker and pour in all of the liquid ingredients.

Shake briefly, strain the liquid into the glass and garnish with the lime slice.

zombie christopher

Since Don Beach's, creation of the original Zombie (the king of cocktails) in 1934, a number of wonderful variations have appeared in the bartenders repertoire. These include the Zombie Prince and this beautifully coloured Zombie Christopher.

Ingredients:

ice cubes

juice of 1 lime

juice of ½ orange

250 ml/8 fl oz pineapple juice

1 measure blue Curaçao

1 measure white rum

1 measure golden rum

½ measure dark rum

Method:

Place some ice cubes in a mixing glass and squeeze over the lime juice, by hand, to release the oil from the skin.

Pour on the remaining ingredients – except the dark rum – and stir vigorously.

Pour the liquid, without straining, into a pre-chilled highball glass, and top with the dark rum.

Stir gently, and garnish with a mint sprig if desired. Serve with a stirrer.

rum cocktails

mai tai

Ingredients:

1 glass crushed ice

1 measure white rum

1 measure dark rum

$^2/_3$ measure triple sec or Cointreau

$^1/_3$ measure orgeat (or amaretto)

$^1/_3$ measure sugar syrup

$^1/_4$ measure grenadine

juice of 1 lime

1 spent lime shell

1 mint sprig

Victor Bergeron, also known as 'Trader Vic', invented the mai tai in 1944, using the finest ingredients that he could find: a mix of 17-year-old J Wray & Nephew rum, triple sec, orgeat, sugar syrup and lime juice. 'Mai tai' is Tahitian for 'the best', and when the drink was introduced to Hawaii in 1953, it was so popular that, within a year, all of the stocks of 17-year-old rum in the world had been exhausted. The cocktail had to be reinvented using a blend of rums.

Method:

Place the crushed ice in a shaker and pour in all of the liquid ingredients. Shake briefly.

Pour the liquid into a Collins glass, add the spent lime shell and garnish with the mint sprig.

Tequila Cocktails

The story goes that the ancient Aztecs were the first to make tequila, producing the pulque (the fermented juice of the agave) after seeing one of the plants being struck by lightening. Later on, the Spanish discovered that they could make this fermented pulque even stronger by distilling it into a spirit. It took a long time for tequila to migrate to the United States, with the first-recorded shipment noted in 1873 and a further three barrels taken home from Mexico by American troops in 1916, following battles with the staunchly teetotal Pancho Villa. Tequila most likely crossed the border during the Prohibition era, but it was only during the 1950s that the drink developed the cult following more associated with the drink today. Many favour the suck-a-lime, knock-back-tequila, lick-salt routine of the tequila slammer, while elsewhere enterprising bartenders have put tequila to new uses in a range of cocktails and mixed drinks.

Tequila is a distillation from a plant – the blue agave – and the spirit must, by law, consist of which 51 per cent of the product. (The remaining 49 per cent is made from cane or other types of sugar.) *Agave tequilana*, a cactus-like plant, is, in fact, a member of the lily family. Its bulbous heart is harvested after eight to ten years' growth, the leaves are removed and the heart is then steam-cooked and crushed. The resulting juice is fermented and distilled in pot stills to produce the spirit.

Clear, white tequila, also known as silver tequila, is matured only for a very short period in stainless-steel or wax-lined vats, which is why it is colourless. (Some lesser brands of white tequila are coloured with caramel to suggest age.) Gold tequila, on the other hand, gets both its name and its colour from maturing in oak vats. If you see gold tequila labelled 'Reposado', it will have been matured in oak tanks for up to six months, while 'Anejo' will have been kept for at least one year – and often two or three, and occasionally eight to ten, years – in oak barrels that were previously used to store bourbon.

Mexican law stipulates that tequila can only be called such if it is produced in a specific geographical area around the town of Tequila. Mescal is a similar drink, distilled from a different variety of agave, but its production is not as tightly controlled, and it does not have the same labelling regulations. It is mescal – and not tequila – that traditionally contains a pickled worm at the bottom of the bottle.

tequila mockingbird

Ingredients:

ice cubes

$1\frac{1}{2}$ measures silver tequila

$\frac{3}{4}$ measure green crème de menthe

$\frac{1}{2}$ measure lime juice

1 lime slice

Time to raise your glass to Harper Lee. Cheers!

Method:

Place some ice cubes in a shaker and pour in the remaining ingredients.

Shake well and strain into a cocktail glass. Garnish with a lime slices.

ambassador

This is a very simple but nevertheless refreshing drink.

Ingredients:

ice cubes

2–4 measures (or more) orange juice

dash of gomme syrup

2 measures tequila

1 orange slice

Method:

Place some ice cubes in a mixing glass and pour in the orange juice, gomme syrup and tequila.

Stir and pour over ice cubes in an old-fashioned glass. Garnish the glass with the orange slice.

tequila cocktails

buttock-clencher

Ingredients:

6 to 8 ice cubes

1 measure silver tequila

1 measure gin

$1/4$ measure melon liqueur

2 measures pineapple juice

2 measures chilled lemonade

2 pineapple cubes

1 maraschino cherry

Many cocktails carry names that were a little risqué for their time, including those that date from the 1920s and 1930s. For example, the mere mention of a 'maiden's kiss' or 'between the sheets' would have brought a blush to many a cheek! And in New York, during the 1930s, the famous French creation, the bloody Mary, was often referred to as a 'red snapper' because the original name was considered offensive!

Method:

Place 3 to 4 ice cubes in a shaker and pour on the tequila, gin, melon liqueur and pineapple juice.

Shake well and strain the liquid into a tall highball glass half-filled with ice.

Top with the chilled lemonade and garnish with pineapple cubes and maraschino cherry on a cocktail stick.

las vegas

Like the town, this cocktail is some way over the top – and completely addictive to boot!

Ingredients:

crushed ice

1½ measures tequila (gold, preferably)

2 measures coconut cream

2 measures orange juice

2 measures pineapple juice

1 measure whipping cream

Method:

Place half a glass of crushed ice in the blender and add the remaining ingredients.

Blend briefly and pour the liquid into a piña colada or hurricane glass.

Garnish with pineapple chunks, if desired.

Replace the tequila with vodka, and you have a Vodka Las Vegas.

tequila cocktails

margarita

The margarita is probably the best-known tequila-based cocktail. It is also one of the most popular, so much so that plenty of young women called Margarita have claimed to be the inspiration for the drink. It is universally accepted, however, that the muse was, in fact, the American actress Marjorie King. Marjorie was a guest at Danny Herrera's Rancho La Gloria in Tijuana in 1948, when he discovered that she was allergic to every spirit except tequila. In mixing this drink for her, he named it after her (Margarita is Spanish for Marjorie). Since then, variations on the original classic recipe have been created, including frozen versions and frozen fruit Margaritas that use fruit liqueurs.

Ingredients:

lime wedge

salt

ice cubes

$\frac{3}{4}$ measure lime juice

$1\frac{1}{4}$ measures triple sec

or Cointreau

2 measures tequila

Method:

Rub the rim of a champagne saucer with a lime wedge and dip the top of the glass into a saucer of salt.

Half-fill a shaker with ice cubes and pour in the lime juice, triple sec or Cointreau and tequila.

Shake well and strain the liquid into the salt-rimmed glass.

earthquake

Ingredients:

2 good scoops crushed ice

1 ½ measures tequila

1 tsp grenadine

2 dashes of Cointreau

2 strawberries

1 orange slice

Variations on the margarita theme abound. This spectacular, frozen, pink version abandons the salt-rimmed glass and is garnished with strawberries instead. It is really easy to prepare in a blender – and in large batches – so makes the perfect drink for a party.

Method:

Place the crushed ice in a blender and pour in the tequila, grenadine and Cointreau.

Mix at high speed for 15 seconds and strain the liquid into a cocktail glass.

Garnish with 2 strawberries and a slice of orange.

el dorado

This drink takes its name from the legendary city of gold sought by Spanish explorers in South America. It is extremely refreshing and you might even be able to pass it off as a honey and vitamin C 'health drink' – if your guests are gullible!

Ingredients:

ice cubes

1 ½ measures lemon juice

1 tablespoon clear honey
(about ½ measure)

2 measures tequila

1 orange slice

Method:

Half-fill a shaker with ice cubes and pour in the lemon juice, honey and tequila.

Shake vigorously and strain the liquid into a Collins glass filled with ice cubes.

Garnish with an orange slice.

tequila cocktails

cactus juice

Ingredients:

1 measure lemon juice

1 teaspoon caster sugar

broken ice cubes

2 measures gold tequila

1 teaspoon Drambuie

This innovative cocktail makes use of Drambuie, Scotland's fine contribution to the world of classic liqueurs. It is a unique blend of whisky, heather, honey and herbs based on a recipe said to have been given as a reward to Captain Mackinon in 1745 following the defeat of Bonnie Prince Charlie at the Battle of Culloden. Mackinon was the protector of the 'Pretender' after the prince was ferried 'over the sea to Skye' and on to safety in France. While the story may be a far-fetched, the Mackinon family continues to make Drambuie in Edinburgh, Scotland.

Method:

First dissolve the sugar in the lemon juice and pour into a shaker with a glassful of broken ice cubes.

Add the tequila and Drambuie and shake well before pouring, unstrained, into an old-fashioned glass.

frozen blue margarita

This is a frozen version of the famous tequila classic and makes for a great way to celebrate the Cinco de Mayo (5th May) in honour of Mexico's national holiday.

Ingredients:

lemon juice

salt

crushed ice and ice cubes

$1\frac{3}{4}$ measures silver tequila

$\frac{3}{4}$ measure blue Curaçao

$\frac{3}{4}$ measure lemon juice

1 lemon slice

Method:

Rub the rim of a large champagne saucer with a little lemon juice, dip the top of the glass in a saucer of salt and fill with crushed ice.

Place the ice cubes in a shaker and pour in the tequila, blue Curaçao and lemon juice.

Shake and strain the drink into the glass . Garnish with a slice of lemon.

tequila cocktails

tequila sunrise

This long, beautifully coloured drink was created in Mexico in the 1930s and has remained incredibly popular ever since. The ingredients are poured straight into a glass and the grenadine is allowed to sink to the bottom. Its stunning!

Ingredients:

ice cubes

4 measures orange juice

2 measures tequila

1/2 measure grenadine

1 orange slice

1 maraschino cherry

Method:

Almost fill a highball glass with ice cubes and pour in the orange juice and tequila.

Stir well and allow to rest before dropping the grenadine into the centre of the drink. Watch it settle to the bottom.

Garnish the glass with an orange slice and a cherry.

tequila moonrise

ice cubes

3 measures tequila

I measure light rum

I measure dark rum

$^1\!/_2$ measure lime cordial

$^1\!/_2$ measure lemon juice

2 measures beer

Once the sun has gone down, you can turn your attention to the moon!

Method:

Half-fill a shaker with ice cubes and pour in the tequila, light and dark rums, lime cordial and lemon juice. Add the sugar.

Shake well and strain the liquid into a Collins glass half-filled with ice cubes.

Top up the glass with the beer.

purple cactus

This drink uses passionfruit juice which brings a quite unique flavour to the mix.

Ingredients:

ice cubes

1 1/2 measures tequila

1 1/2 measures passionfruit juice

1/2 measure sherry

1 teaspoon grenadine

broken ice

1 maraschino cherry on a stick

Method:

Half-fill a shaker with ice cubes and pour in the tequila, passionfruit juice, sherry and grenadine.

Shake well and strain the liquid into an old-fashioned glass three-quarters filled with broken ice.

Garnish the drink with the cherry on a stick.

tequila cocktails

mexicano

Pineapple juice is the perfect partner for tequila, and makes a cocktail go down nice and smoothly.

Ingredients:

ice cubes

1 measure pineapple juice

1/2 measure lemon juice

1 teaspoon grenadine

2 measures tequila

Method:

Half-fill a shaker with ice cubes and pour in the pineapple juice, lemon juice, grenadine and tequila.

Shake well and strain the liquid into a cocktail glass.

frozen matador

This is a very simple cocktail to make – a mix of crushed ice, tequila and pineapple juice – with frothy and refreshing results. Using a blender, it is easy to prepare in large quantities, making a great drink for long, hot summer days with friends and neighbours.

Ingredients:

2 good scoops crushed ice

dash of lime juice

1 measure pineapple juice

1 measure tequila

2 ice cubes

2 pineapple chunks

2 to 3 mint leaves

Method:

Place the crushed ice in a blender and pour in the lime juice, pineapple juice and tequila.

Blend the ingredients to a frothy mix and strain into a rocks glass over two ice cubes.

Garnish with the pineapple chunks and mint leaves.

tequila cocktails

midori margarita

Ingredients:

lemon juice

salt

3 to 4 ice cubes

1 measure white or silver tequila

1 tbsp lime juice

1 measure Midori

There are countless variations of the original margarita, created by Danny Herrera at his Rancho del Gloria restaurant near Tijuana, New Mexico. First made in 1948, the drink was inspired by the actress Marjorie King.

Today you will find a blue margarita, a Galliano margarita and a golden margarita. There are also frozen-fruit margaritas, which are served over crushed ice. Tequila is the common link, and the famously salted (or sugared) rim of the cocktail glass. This variation uses Midori, a vibrant-green, melon liqueur from Japan.

Method:

Chill a champagne saucer, then moisten the rim with lemon juice and dip the top of the glass into a saucer of salt.

Place the ice in a shaker and pour in the tequila, lime juice and Midori.

Shake and strain the liquid into the salt-rimmed glass.

Brandy Cocktails

Brandy, is a warming, sensual spirit distilled from wine, and is produced in many countries throughout the world. Consequently it takes several forms and its origins are disputed. Some say that brandy was first discovered in France during the 13th century, the result of various attempts to make a medicinal drink; others claim that a 15th-century alchemist buried his barrel of precious *aqua vitae* in his garden in a bid to keep it out of the hands of looting soldiers. Unfortunately, however, he was killed before returning to it, and his barrel remained undiscovered until many years later. By that time, half of the liquor had evaporated, but what remained was rich and smooth.

Brandy generally undergoes two distillations, which results in a clear, colourless spirit. This is then aged in oak barrels, during which gives the drink takes on its nut-brown colour and rich flavour. The longer the brandy ages, the more refined its flavour. The king of brandies is cognac, which hails from a specific area centred on the town of Cognac, in the Charentes region of France. To be recognised as a true cognac, French law dictates that the brandy may only be made from specified white grapes grown and distilled in a given area. Twice distilled and aged in oak barrels for at least two years, the end result is 80 per cent alcohol by volume (abv). Cognac is sold under various ratings. Three stars, or 'VS', mean that the cognac has matured for two years in the barrel; 'VSOP', 'Vieux', 'VO' and 'reserve' mean that the cognac has aged in the barrel for at least four years; 'VVSOP' and 'Grand Reserve' denote cognacs that have matured in the barrel for at least five years; and 'Extra', 'Napoleon', 'XO', Très Vieux' and 'Vieille reserve' all denote cognacs that have aged for between six and ten years in their barrels.

Armagnac is a pale-golden-coloured French brandy with a dry, fiery taste, and can only be made using white grapes from the Haute-Armagnac, Tenareze and Bas-Armagnac regions of Gascony. The distillation takes place after the grape harvest (from October to April), and, unlike cognac, armagnac has only one distillation (although recently French law has been relaxed to allow double distillation, which speeds up the ageing process that occurs in oak barrels). Three stars on the label mean that it has been matured for at least two years; 'VSOP', for at least five years; 'Napoleon' and 'XO', for at least six years; and 'Hors d'Age' means that it has aged for at least ten years in the barrel. A vintage year on the label indicates the year of harvest.

Outside France, brandy is produced wherever grapes are grown, and you will find fine examples in both the Old World of Spain, Portugal, Italy, Greece and Germany, and the New World, particularly in California, in the United States, and in Chile, in South America.

corpse reviver

Ingredients:

3 to 4 ice cubes

1 measure brandy

⅔ measure sweet vermouth

⅔ measure Calvados

Traditionally an early-morning pick-me-up, this inspired cocktail was created by Frank Meier at the Ritz Bar in Paris in the 1920s. The Savoy Cocktail Book stated that it should be drunk "before 11 am, or whenever steam and energy are needed"!

Method:

Place the ice cubes in a mixing glass and pour in the remaining ingredients.

Stir and strain into a pre-chilled cocktail glass.

pisco sour

What better opportunity to try out pisco, a colourless brandy from South America?

Ingredients:

broken ice

juice of ½ lime

ice cubes

2 measures pisco

1 teaspoon sugar syrup

½ an egg white

1 dash angostura bitters

sprig of mint

Method:

Fill an old-fashioned glass with broken ice and squeeze in the juice of the ½ a lime, by hand.

Place the remaining ingredients in a shaker with some ice cubes and shake well.

Strain the liquid into the ice-filled glass and garnish with a sprig of mint.

brandy cocktails

betsy ross

This all-American cocktail is named after Betsy Griscom Ross (1752–1836), who made the very first United States flag.

Ingredients:

ice cubes

2 measures brandy

1 measure port

½ teaspoon triple sec or Cointreau

1 dash bitters

Method:

Place some ice cubes in a mixing glass and pour in the brandy, port, triple sec or Cointreau and bitters.

Stir well and strain the liquid into an old-fashioned glass filled with ice cubes.

charles cocktail

This is a simple enough recipe and yet it packs a powerful punch!

Ingredients:

ice cubes

2 measures brandy

$\frac{1}{2}$ measure rosso vermouth

2 dashes bitters

Method:

Place some ice cubes in a mixing glass and pour in the brandy and rosso vermouth.

Add the bitters and stir well before straining into a pre-chilled cocktail glass.

brandy cocktails

brandy cocktails

ritz cocktail

Ingredients:

3 to 4 ice cubes

$^3/_4$ measure brandy or cognac

$^3/_4$ measure Cointreau

$^3/_4$ measure orange juice

chilled champagne (or sparkling white wine), as required

1 orange slice

This is a wonderfully aromatic champagne cocktail that makes a perfect choice for an apéritif or after-dinner drink. Actually, it's so good that you can drink it any time the mood takes you!

Method:

Place the ice cubes in a shaker and pour in the brandy, Cointreau and orange juice.

Shake and strain into a champagne flute.

Top up with chilled champagne and garnish the glass with the orange slice.

b & b

The 'B's in this cocktail should be obvious: one is for Benedictine the other for brandy (preferably cognac). Benedictine was first made in 1510, by Benedictine monks at their abbey at Fécamp, in Normandy, France. The production process involves using some 27 herbs, plants, fruit peels and flowers, takes three years and is completed only after a further four years of ageing. It makes the perfect partner to a good brandy.

Ingredients:

3 to 4 ice cubes

1 measure brandy or cognac

1 measure Benedictine

Method:

Place all of the ingredients in a mixing glass and stir.

Strain the liquid into a liqueur or cordial glass.

b & b
collins

It is thought that the Collins got its name from one John Collins – a famous head waiter at Limmers, a London coffee house and hotel situated in Conduit Street from 1790 to 1817. The original version is made using gin, while this one is made with brandy, and a little Benedictine sprinkled over the top.

Ingredients:

2 good scoops crushed ice

2 measures brandy or cognac

juice of $\frac{1}{2}$ lemon

1 tsp sugar syrup

chilled soda water, as required

1 measure Benedictine

1 lemon slice

1 cocktail cherry

Method:

Place the crushed ice in a mixing glass and pour in the brandy, lemon juice and sugar syrup.

Stir well, strain the liquid into a chilled Collins or highball glass and top with chilled soda water.

Carefully float the Benedictine on the surface and garnish with a slice of lemon and a cherry.

brandy cocktails

metropolitan

Ingredients:

crushed ice

1/2 measure rosso vermouth

1 teaspoon caster sugar

1 dash bitters

2 measures brandy

A fitting toast to any great city!

Method:

Half-fill a shaker with crushed ice and pour in the rosso vermouth, sugar, dash of bitters and the brandy.

Shake well and strain into a cocktail glass.

lord chamberlain

This cocktail is named after the head of the Queen of England's household – and a heady mix it is!

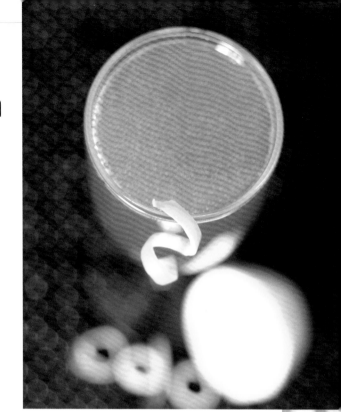

Ingredients:

ice cubes

1 measure dry vermouth

1 measure port

3 drops bitters

2 measures brandy

1 lemon twist

Method:

Place some ice cubes in a mixing glass and pour in the vermouth and port.

Add the bitters and then pour in the brandy.

Stir well and strain into a pre-chilled cocktail glass.

Add a twist of lemon.

brandy cocktails

sidecar

Ingredients:

2 to 3 ice cubes

1 1/2 measures brandy or cognac

1 measure Cointreau

1 measure lemon juice (or more to taste)

Great as an apéritif, this cocktail has a certain sharpness to it. It is supposedly named after the somewhat eccentric, military man who invented it, and who is said to have arrived habitually at Harry's New York Bar, in Paris, France, in the sidecar of his own chauffeur-driven motorcycle.

Method:

Place the ice cubes in a shaker and pour in the brandy, Cointreau and lemon juice.

Shake and then strain the liquid into a cocktail glass.

cherry blossom

A number of variations of this cocktail exist, one of which has nothing to do with cherries, while another is made with gin. This version involves cherry brandy as well as cognac, and a dash or two of grenadine for a deeper red. In some bars, the rim of the glass is dipped in cherry brandy and then into sugar, which may appeal if you have an extra-sweet tooth.

Ingredients:

3 to 4 ice cubes

$^3/_4$ measure cognac

$^3/_4$ measure cherry brandy

$^3/_4$ measure lemon juice

2 tsps Cointreau

2 tsps grenadine

2 maraschino cherries

Method:

Place the ice in a shaker and pour in all of the liquid ingredients.

Shake and strain into a pre-chilled cocktail glass.

Pop the maraschino cherries on a cocktail stick to garnish the glass.

brandy cocktails

brandy alexander

Despite its incredibly simple construction, the brandy-based Alexander has become one of the most sophisticated after-dinner cocktails of all time. Not only that, but there are now a number of different versions to choose from, ranging from the coffee Alexander and Alexander's sister, a treat for mint-lovers.

Ingredients:

2 to 3 ice cubes

$1\frac{1}{3}$ measures dark crème de cacao

$1\frac{1}{3}$ measures double cream

$1\frac{1}{3}$ measures brandy

grated chocolate or nutmeg

Method:

Place the ice cubes in a shaker and add the crème de cacao and the cream.

Pour in the brandy and shake well.

Strain the liquid into a cocktail glass or champagne saucer and sprinkle the top with grated chocolate or nutmeg.

between the sheets

Ingredients:

3 to 4 ice cubes

1 ½ measures cognac

1 measure light rum

1 measure Cointreau

1 dash lemon juice

This classic cocktail from the 1930s, has a slightly risqué name and a tangy, fruity taste to match. It makes for a perfect drink for the evening: pre-dinner, pre-theatre or, perhaps, even pre-bedtime!

Method:

Place the ice in a shaker and pour in the remaining ingredients.

Shake and strain into a cocktail glass.

stinger

Like many famous cocktails, this true classic originated in America's Prohibition era. Served straight up originally, it is now popular as a sipping drink on the rocks. It takes no time at all to put together, its spicy freshness bringing the perfect end an evening meal.

Ingredients:

3 to 4 ice cubes

1 1/2 measures brandy or cognac

3/4 measure white crème de menthe

Method:

Place the ice cubes in a mixing glass and pour in the brandy and crème de menthe.

Stir and strain the liquid into a pre-chilled cocktail glass.

brandy cocktails

st. kitts

Ingredients:

ice cubes

1 1/2 measures grapefruit juice

1 measure dry vermouth

3 measures brandy

1 maraschino cherry

This fruity number is named after
the island of St Kitts in the
Leeward Islands
of the eastern West Indies.

Method:

Half-fill a shaker with ice cubes.

Pour in the grapefruit juice, vermouth and brandy.

Shake well and strain into a cocktail glass.

Garnish with a maraschino cherry.

Wine & Champagne Cocktails

There are four main wine categories: still wine; sparkling wine; fortified wine and aromatised wine, and the recipes in this section give you the perfect opportunity to use all of them. Still wine can be red, white or rosé. Each can also be dry, medium dry or sweet. Since, when making cocktails, wine is mixed with other flavourings and liqueurs, there is no real point in choosing a wine of exceptional quality, which is best enjoyed on its own.

The undoubted 'queen' of sparkling wines is, of course, champagne. To earn the name the wine must come from the designated region in France, 160km (100 miles) north of Paris, around Rheims and Épernay. However, other fine sparkling wines – what the French call *vins mousseux* and the Italians call *spumante* – are made outside the region and outside France. Champagne should be served thoroughly chilled, but not icy. While champagne is a must for really special occasions, you should also try some of the great sparkling wines from California, Australia, Spain, Italy and France once in a while.

Fortified wines are those that have had brandy added to them, port and sherry being two best-known types available. Port originates from the Douro region of Portugal. The brandy added to the wine stops the process of fermentation, leaving some of the sugar behind, which results in the sweet fortified wine. Vintage port has been declared by the maker as being good enough to be called vintage and must be bottled within two years and then aged in the bottle for between 8 and 20 years. Tawny port is aged in the barrel and is clarified of sediment by using egg whites. During this process, the wood removes some of the colour of the port: the longer it is aged, the paler (tawnier) and drier the port becomes. A good tawny port is perfect for making many of the mixed drinks offered here. Ruby port is aged for less time and consequently keeps some of its colour and its full body. White port is drier than the other ports and is made only from white grapes, although it is still barrel-aged.

Sherry is the English name for the Spanish Jerez, which comes from the town of the same name in the Cadiz region of Andalusia. It is only a true sherry if it is made in the Jerez region, although several other countries (such as South Africa and Cyprus) also produce versions. The wine is placed in casks in order for a yeast scum – called flor – to develop. This is caused by natural airborne yeast and growth is variable. The amount of flor that develops governs the type of sherry produced. At this point, the wine is fortified with brandy. Aromatised wines were originally sour wines sweetened with honey and herbs to make them more palatable. They are generally quite sweet, and contain a high proportion of mistelle (brandy mixed with grape juice). Some of the most popular aromatised wines are Campari, and vermouth.

Cocktail Heaven   133

ritz fizz

This beautiful champagne makes a
delicious contribution to any
celebration – an engagement, a
wedding, an anniversary, a birthday
– or just for dinner à deux perhaps!

Ingredients:

1 teaspoon filtered lemon juice

1 teaspoon blue Curaçao

1 teaspoon amaretto

3½ measures champagne

1 rose petal

Method:

Pour each of the ingredients to a pre-chilled

champagne flute and float a small rose petal

on top.

hillary wallbanger

Time to meet Harvey's cousin!

Ingredients:

ice cubes

4 measures dry white wine

2 measures orange juice

1/2 measure Galliano

Method:

Fill a Collins glass two-thirds full with ice cubes.

Pour in the white wine and orange juice and stir well.

Float the Galliano on top before serving, and drop in a cherry, if desired.

classic
champagne cocktail

In 1889, John Dougherty was awarded a gold medal in New York, for his cocktail recipe. In actual fact, he had come across the recipe twenty-five years earlier, in the Southern states of America, at which time it had a dash of spring water added. The true origins of the cocktail continue to remain a mystery to this day.

Ingredients:

1 sugar cube

2 dashes angostura bitters

$^1/_3$ measure cognac

3 measures chilled champagne

1 thin strip lemon peel

1 orange slice

Method:

Drop the sugar cube into a champagne flute and add the angostura bitters. Let the sugar cube soak them up.

Pour in the cognac and then add the champagne.

Twist the lemon peel over the top of the glass to release the oil, and then discard it.

Garnish the glass with the orange slice.

For more kick, add $^1/_3$ measure Grand Marnier and a dash of sugar syrup.

mimosa

Ingredients:

3 measures orange juice

3 measures chilled champagne

1 orange twist

1 orange slice

This cocktail is a delicious 50:50 mix of champagne and orange juice and was created in 1925 at the Ritz Hotel in Paris. It takes its name from the beautiful tropical flower whose colour it resembles.

Method:

Pour the orange juice and champagne into a pre-chilled champagne flute.

Add the slice of orange and garnish .

Add $^1/2$ measure Cointreau and you have a grand mimosa.

diplomatic answer

This 'diplomatic answer' combines vermouth, which is generally considered an aperitif, with brandy, typically a digestif. It makes for a great herb- and orange-flavoured long drink that you can drink at any time of day.

Ingredients:

broken ice

2 measures rosso vermouth

1 measure brandy

$\frac{1}{3}$ measure triple sec or Cointreau

4 measures lemonade

1 orange slice

Method:

Half-fill a large wine glass with broken ice.

Pour in the vermouth, brandy and triple sec and top up the glass with lemonade.

Garnish the glass with the slice of orange.

wine & champagne cocktails

kir royale

Ingredients:

$^1/_3$ measure crème de cassis

$4^1/_2$ measures chilled champagne

This regal cocktail combines crème de cassis with the 'king of wines' champagne. The blackcurrant liqueur is a speciality of the Burgundy region of France. When added to white Burgundy wine, it makes a simple 'kir', named after Canon Kir, a wartime mayor of Dijon and left-wing politician.

Method:

Pour the crème de cassis into a pre-chilled champagne flute and add the champagne.

hotel california

This is a very refreshing fruit-flavoured cocktail. Its American west-coast origins are clear from the use of tequila, which is made from the fermented and distilled juice of the agave in nearby Mexico.

Ingredients:

6 to 8 ice cubes

2 measures pineapple juice

2 measures mandarin juice

1 measure gold tequila

4 measures chilled champagne

Method:

Put 2 to 3 ice cubes into a shaker and pour in the juices and the tequila.

Shake and strain into a poco glass or goblet filled with the remaining ice and top with the champagne.

Serve with a straw or two.

wine & champagne cocktails

champagne charlie

Ingredients:

1 scoop broken ice

1 measure apricot brandy

4 measures chilled champagne (preferably Charles Heidsieck)

$^1/_2$ orange slice

The 'charlie' in this cocktail is Monsieur Charles-Camille Heidsieck, who began producing champagne in 1851. He was a consummate salesman, as well as a celebrated *bon viveur*, which is how the nickname 'Champagne Charlie' came about.

Method:

Place the broken ice into a pre-chilled wine glass and pour in the apricot brandy.

Add the champagne and garnish the glass with the $^1/_2$ slice of orange.

ritz bar fizz

This fun and fruity cocktail was created at the Ritz Bar of the Ritz-Carlton Hotel in Boston, Massachusetts.

Ingredients:

1 measure grapefruit juice

1 measure pineapple juice

3 measures chilled champagne

1 teaspoon grenadine

1 maraschino cherry

1 sprig of mint

Method:

Pour the grapefruit and pineapple juices into a pre-chilled champagne saucer.

Add the chilled champagne, followed by the grenadine.

Garnish with a cherry and a sprig of mint.

wine & champagne cocktails

bellini

Ingredients:

1 large peach, skinned and puréed to make 1½ measures peach juice

1 teaspoon gomme syrup

3 measures champagne – thoroughly chilled

1 strawberry (optional)

Legendary bartender Guiseppe Cipriani created this champagne and peach-juice cocktail at Harry's Bar in Venice in 1943. It marked a major exhibition celebrating the work of one of the city's most famous sons, the Renaissance painter Giovanni Bellini (c. 1430–1516).

Method:

Skin the peach and purée it in a blender or food processor. This should give you enough purée for 1½ measures.

Pour the purée/juice into a pre-chilled champagne flute and add the gomme syrup.

Pour in the champagne and garnish with a strawberry, if desired.

mango bellini

Ingredients:

1 ¹/₂ measures mango juice

1 tsp sugar syrup

3 measures chilled champagne

1 lemon slice

1 cherry

This cocktail is a modern rendition of the world-famous bellini, created by Giuseppi Cipriani in 1943, to celebrate an exhibition of the Venetian artist, Bellini. While the classic version uses peach juice, this contemporary take on the drink uses mango juice.

Method:

Mix the mango juice and sugar syrup together and pour into a pre-chilled champagne flute.

Pour in the champagne and garnish the with a slice of lemon and a cherry.

texas fizz

Like all fizz recipes, this one was originally made with soda water, and later upgraded to champagne. An extra kick comes from the gin, while the grenadine and orange juice add fruitiness, and turn this long drink the colour of a stunning Texas sunset.

Ingredients:

3 to 4 ice cubes

1 measure orange juice

$^1/_4$ measure grenadine

1 measure gin

1 scoop broken ice

4 measures chilled champagne

1 orange slice

Method:

Place the ice cubes in a shaker and pour in the orange juice, grenadine and gin.

Strain the liquid into a highball glass three-quarters filled with broken ice and add the champagne.

Garnish the drink with the slice of orange.

wine & champagne cocktails

americano

While this is one of the classiest aperitifs of all time, it is very simple to make well. It is also a great drink to have while indulging in that Italian pastime of 'people watching'.

Ingredients:

ice cubes

1½ measures rosso vermouth

1½ measures Campari

1 twist each of lemon and orange

soda water to taste

1 orange slice

Method:

Half-fill a highball glass with ice cubes and pour in the vermouth, then the Campari.

Add the twists of lemon and orange and stir well.

Top with soda water to taste, and garnish the glass with the slice of orange.

blue splash

Blue Curaçao made a real splash when it first became available during the 1960s. Bartenders around the world began devising gorgeously coloured cocktails and mixed drinks that showed off its colour to real advantage. Like other Curaçaos, this has an orange flavour. The blue splash is a fruity, sparkling drink that is great for parties. You could use sparkling white wine instead of champagne, and it would still taste wonderful!

Ingredients:

3 to 4 ice cubes

$^3/_4$ measure gin

$^3/_4$ measure blue Curaçao

$^3/_4$ measure lemon juice

2 tsps dry vermouth

1 dash angostura bitters

champagne or sparkling white wine, as required

$^1/_2$ orange slice

Method:

Place the ice cubes in a mixing glass and pour in all of the remaining ingredients except for the champagne and orange garnish.

Strain the liquid into a rocks glass and top up with champagne.

Garnish the glass with the half orange slice.

Liqueur Cocktails

The word 'liqueur' has various meanings, depending where you are. In France, it is any after-dinner drink, such as liqueur brandy. In Britain, a liqueur is a sweetish drink made from a base spirit into which flavouring agents, such as roots, fruits, seeds, barks and flowers, have been infused, macerated or redistilled. To an American, liqueurs are called cordials (while, in Britain, these are flavoured syrups, with little or no alcohol in them).

Liqueurs are among the oldest forms of alcoholic drinks. Monks in religious fraternities used to work with herbs to exploit their medicinal properties and were among the first to produce liqueurs in the process. They usually achieved this by adding honey or sugar to sweeten the bitter elixirs that they had made for their patients. Two of the most famous of these 'holy elixirs' are Chartreuse and Benedictine. The former, made originally by Carthusian monks at the monastery of La Grande Chartreuse, near Grenoble, France, dates back to the early 16th century and contains 130 herbs and spices. Having perfected the maceration, infusion and distillation process in 1764, commercial production began in 1848. When, at one stage, the monks were exiled to Spain, they began a distillery in Tarragona. Only three monks know the secret recipe at any one time, and they visit the Spainsh distillery three times a year to oversee production. There are two forms of Chartreuse: a mild yellow Chartreuse and a spicier, and more powerful, green Chartreuse.

Benedictine dates from 1510 and is often described as the world's oldest liqueur. The amber-coloured liqueur originated in the abbey at Fécamp in Normandy, northern France. The abbey was sacked during the French Revolution, and, in 1863, the secret formula passed into the hands of a local merchant called Alexander Le Grand, said to be a descendent of a trustee of the abbey. Le Grand recreated the elixir, which contains 27 herbs, plants, flowers and fruit peels, and each bottle is still emblazoned with the motto *Deo Optimo Maximo* ('To God Most Good, Most Great').

Liqueurs come in an enormous range of flavours, from mint to chocolate, and from nut to coffee. Some of the most frequently used in cocktails are those called 'crème'. In spite of their name, they do not usually contain cream, but consist mostly of cognac or brandy, plus the flavour. There is, for instance, crème de banane (banana); crème de cacao (chocolate), crème de menthe (mint), crème de cassis (blackcurrant), fraise (strawberry), and framboise (raspberry).

Cocktail Heaven   151

white lady cocktail

The original white lady was created by Harry MacElhone at Ciro's Club, in London, in 1919. Harry later changed the recipe at his own bar in Paris, in 1929, replacing the white crème de menthe with gin.

Ingredients:

ice cubes

1 measure lemon juice

1 measure white crème de menthe

1 measure Cointreau

Method:

Place the ice cubes in a shaker and pour in the remaining ingredients.

Shake well and strain into a cocktail glass.

blue cloud cocktail

This fun cocktail really does look like a blue sky with fluffy white clouds!

Ingredients:

1 measure amaretto

½ measure blue Curaçao

2 measures vanilla ice cream

1 spoonful whipped cream

1 cherry

Method:

Combine the amaretto, blue Curaçao and vanilla ice cream in a blender and blend until smooth – it should be the consistency of a thick milkshake.

Pour the drink into brandy snifter and top with whipped cream and the cherry.

liqueur cocktails

gemini

This cocktail uses Grand Marnier, which makes use of Caribbean bitter oranges steeped in cognac. There are two varieties of the liqueur available: the clear Grand Marnier used here, and a red variety called Grand Marnier Cordon Rouge. The Galliano adds a flowery, yet spicy, note to the mix.

Ingredients:

1 scoop broken ice

1 measure chilled orange juice

$^{1}/_{2}$ measure cognac

$^{3}/_{4}$ measure Grand Marnier

$^{3}/_{4}$ measure Galliano

1 strip orange peel

Method:

Fill a rocks glass two-thirds full with broken ice and pour in the orange juice, cognac, Grand Marnier and Galliano. Stir briefly.

Twist the strip of orange peel over the drink to release its oil and discard the peel before serving the cocktail.

blushin' russian

The Russian in this cocktail comes from the vodka, and the blush from the strawberry!

Ingredients:

1 measure coffee liqueur such as Tia Maria or kahlua

¾ measure vodka

1 scoop vanilla ice cream

5 large fresh strawberries

Method:

Set the best-looking strawberry aside for garnish.

Combine the remaining ingredients in a blender and blend until smooth.

Pour into a pre-chilled parfait or white wine glass and garnish with the strawberry.

liqueur cocktails

snowball

Many consider the the snowball to be a 'girlie' drink. This is largely because most people are deceived by the taste and think the drink has a low alcohol content. In fact the average alcohol content is about two units, and there's nothing girlie about that!

Ingredients:

ice cubes

2 measures Advocaat

$1/4$ measure lime cordial

5 measures chilled lemonade

1 cherry

Method:

Place some ice cubes in a Collins or highball glass, and pour in the Advocaat.

Add the lime cordial and top up the glass with chilled lemonade.

Garnish the drink with a cherry on a stick and serve with straws and a stirrer.

velvet hammer

Several versions of this delicious drink exist, and here are two to try. Common to both of them is the Cointreau and the use of a coffee-flavoured liqueur. The best known of the latter are Kahlua, from Mexico, and Tia Maria, from Jamaica.

Ingredients:

Velvet hammer 1

3 to 4 ice cubes

$^3/_4$ measure Tia Maria or Kahlua

$^3/_4$ measure Cointreau

$^3/_4$ measure single cream

Velvet hammer 2

3 to 4 ice cubes

1 measure Tia Maria or Kahlua

1 measure Cointreau

$^1/_2$ measure brandy

1 measure whipping cream

1 scoop broken ice

1 cherry, to garnish

Method:

To make velvet hammer 1, shake the ingredients in a shaker and strain the liquid into a cocktail glass.

For velvet hammer 2, place some ice cubes in a shaker and add all of the remaining ingredients, except for the broken ice and the cherry.

Shake and strain the liquid into a rocks glass filled with broken ice. Garnish with the cherry.

liqueur cocktails

grasshopper

Ingredients:

3 to 4 ice cubes

1 $\frac{1}{3}$ measures white crème de cacao

1 measure green crème de menthe

1 $\frac{1}{3}$ measures whipping cream

grated chocolate

1 mint sprig

This popular, vivid-green drink is a blend of whipped cream, chocolate and mint, which makes the perfect after-dinner combination. The word *Chouao* on the label of crème de cacao indicates that the cocoa beans used in making the product came from Venezuela, Chouao being a suburb of the city of Caracas.

Method:

Place the ice in a shaker and pour over the crème de cacao, crème de menthe and the cream.

Shake vigorously and strain the liquid into a pre-chilled champagne saucer. Garnish with some grated chocolate and a mint sprig.

For a flying grasshopper, use 1 measure white crème de cacao, 1 measure vodka and $\frac{1}{3}$ measure green crème de menthe. Shake briefly with $\frac{3}{4}$ glassful of crushed ice and pour, unstrained, into a rocks glass.

sex on the beach

This is one of those drinks that everyone knows the name of, but not many dare to order! Now's your chance to try it in the privacy of your own home with a handful or your very closest friends!

Ingredients:

2 to 3 ice cubes

$\frac{1}{2}$ measure crème de framboise (raspberry liqueur)

$\frac{1}{2}$ measure Midori (melon liqueur)

$\frac{1}{2}$ measure vodka

1 measure pineapple juice

cranberry juice

Method:

Place the ice cubes in a mixing glass and pour in the remaining ingredients except the cranberry juice.

Stir and strain the liquid into cordial glass.

Top up with cranberry juice.

galliano stinger

Originally, stingers were very refreshing, spicy drinks that were served straight up. During the Prohibition era in the US, however, they became popular served over crushed ice. The crème de menthe provides the 'sting' in this Galliano-based mix, Galliano itself being a liqueur that rose to fame in the harvey wallbanger during the 1950s.

Ingredients:

2 to 3 ice cubes

1 1/2 measures Galliano

3/4 measure white crème de menthe

1 scoop crushed ice (optional)

Method:

Place the ice cubes in a shaker, pour in the Galliano and white crème de menthe and shake. Strain into a cocktail glass if you want the drink straight up, or strain over crushed ice in a champagne saucer.

To make a comfortable stinger, use 1 1/2 measures Southern Comfort; for a Roman stinger, use 3/4 measure sambuca and 3/4 measure cognac; and for a bee stinger, use 1 1/2 measures blackberry brandy.

liqueur cocktails

liqueur cocktails

cool operator

This fruity little number certainly has a laid-back feel to it!

Ingredients:

ice cubes

1 measure Midori melon liqueur

½ measure lime juice

½ measure vodka

½ measure light rum

4 measures grapefruit juice

2 measures orange juice

1 cherry

Method:

Place some ice in a blender and pour in the remaining ingredients.

Blend until thick and pour the liquid into a pre-chilled parfait or white wine glass.

Garnish with a cherry on a stick.

midori sour

The invention of the sour dates back to the 1850s, but it was not until a century or so later that the Japanese distiller Sun-Tory developed its bright-green, melon liqueur called Midori.

Ingredients:

2 to 3 ice cubes

1 $\frac{1}{2}$ measures Midori

1 measure lemon juice

$\frac{1}{2}$ measure sugar syrup

1 scoop broken ice

chilled soda water (optional)

2 pineapple chunks

1 cherry

Method:

Place the ice cubes in a shaker and add the Midori, lemon juice and sugar syrup.

Shake and then strain the liquid into a rocks glass two-thirds full with broken ice.

Top with a splash of soda water, if desired, and garnish the glass the fruit.

For a raspberry sour, use 1 $\frac{1}{2}$ measures Chambord and $\frac{1}{2}$ measure white rum; for an amaretto sour, use 1 $\frac{1}{2}$ measures amaretto.

liqueur cocktails

chartreuse cocktail

This is a simple cocktail using the yellow version of this famous French liqueur.

Ingredients:

ice cubes

1 measure yellow Chartreuse

1 measure cognac

$^1/_2$ measure dry vermouth

1 cherry

Method:

Place the ice cubes in a mixing glass and pour in the Chartreuse, cognac and vermouth.

Stir and strain the liquid into a liqueur or cordial glass and garnish with a cherry.

Calvados Cocktails

Almost any fruit can be enjoyed in alcoholic form, although some fruits are more suitable than others. It is often a question of the fruit's sugar content.

Calvados, is an apple brandy made from the cider produced in Normandy, France. Under strict French laws, the name 'Calvados' can only be applied to the cider distillations that come from just 11 specified areas. After distillation, the liquid is stored in oak or chestnut barrels and matured for at least two years. Generally, the older the Calvados is, the more amber-brown its colour, and the more velvety and aromatic its taste. This fine spirit is rarely drunk to accompany meals in France, but is often served between courses at formal dinner parties as an aid to digestion and for pepping up the appetite, ready to tackle the remaining dishes of the feast! For many French lovers of the drink, Calvados might be the last drink of the day, or, indeed, the first: café-Calva, a strong coffee with Calvados on the side, or strong coffee fortified with Calvados, is not uncommon.

As in the case for cognac (and armagnac), Calvados is distinguished by a labelling system that indicates the number of years that it has been aged in the barrel: three stars means two years at least; 'Vieux' and 'Reserve' indicate at least three years; 'VO', 'Vieille Reserve' or 'VSOP' guarantee at least four years' maturation; while 'Extra' or 'XO', 'Napoleon', 'Hors d'Age' and 'Age Inconnu' (literally, 'unknown age') indicate that the Calvados has been maturing in its barrel for at least six years.

Calvados is not the only form of apple brandy. There are many others that cannot be called Calvados, but are nevertheless fine products. These apple brandies, including French products made outside the controlled regions, are known as *eaux-de-vie de pomme* ('the water of life of apples'). Applejack is a delightful, American apple brandy, and a speciality of New England, while *aquardiente di sidre* is a version that comes from Spain. Austria and Germany have *Obstler*, which is made from fermented apples (or pears, or a mixture of the two). In all cases, the variety of fruit must be listed on the label, and the majority of these brandies boast between 80 and 100 per cent alcohol by volume (abv).

Young Calvados, applejack and apple brandies in general are increasingly popular when drunk on the rocks or in cocktails, and this section has a few recipes for you to try for yourself.

angel face

A heavenly blend of gin, apricot brandy and Calvados.

Ingredients:

ice cubes

1 measure gin

1 measure apricot brandy

1 measure Calvados

Method:

Place the ice cubes in a shaker and pour over the remaining ingredients.

Shake vigorously and strain into a pre-chilled cocktail glass.

calvados sour

Sours came into being during the 1850s, with the creation of the whiskey sour. These drinks were very popular, and were even served in their own, stemmed glass, although today they are more likely to be served in a rocks or old-fashioned glass. Soda water found its way into the drink in the 1880s, but always as an option.

Ingredients:

6 to 8 ice cubes

$^3/_4$ measure lemon juice

2 tsps sugar syrup

$1^1/_2$ measures Calvados

1 orange slice

1 maraschino cherry

chilled, sparkling, mineral water, as required (optional)

Method:

Half-fill a rocks glass with ice.

Place the remaining ice in a shaker and pour in the lemon juice, sugar syrup and Calvados.

Shake well and strain the liquid into the rocks glass.

Garnish the glass with the $^1/_2$ slice of orange and the maraschino cherry.

Top with a mineral water, if desired.

calvados cocktails

vermont

Vermont is known for its Green Mountains, a range popular for winter sports. This fruity mix of apple brandy and grenadine is ideal for après-ski or following a hearty, New England supper.

Ingredients:

3 to 4 ice cubes

$1\frac{1}{2}$ measures Calvados or applejack

2 tsps grenadine

2 tsps lemon juice

Method:

Place all of the ingredients in a shaker and shake well.

Strain the liquid into a cocktail glass.

apple blossom

This fresh mix is a variation of the cognac-based cherry blossom. The cocktail uses maple syrup as its sweetener, which is widely available outside North America.

Ingredients:

1 good scoop crushed ice

1 measure Calvados or applejack

$^3/_4$ measure apple juice

1 tbsp maple syrup

2 tsps lemon juice

$^1/_2$ slice lemon, to garnish

Method:

Place the crushed ice in a blender and pour in the Calvados, apple juice, maple syrup and lemon juice.

Whizz briefly and pour the liquid into a pre-chilled champagne saucer.

Garnish the edge of the glass with a lemon slice.

calvados cocktails

calvados cocktail

A number of versions of this cocktail exist, and two are given here. The first version is fruity and slightly sweet, while the second is a little milder in taste. Try them both to find the one you like best. Calvados cocktail 1 is pictured.

Ingredients:

Calvados cocktail 1

3 to 4 ice cubes

$1\frac{1}{2}$ measures Calvados

$\frac{3}{4}$ measure grenadine

$\frac{3}{4}$ measure orange juice

1 dash orange bitters

Calvados cocktail 2

3 to 4 ice cubes

$\frac{3}{4}$ measure Calvados

$\frac{3}{4}$ measure Grand Marnier

$\frac{3}{4}$ measure orange juice

$\frac{1}{2}$ orange slice

Method:

Shake all of the liquid ingredients together in a shaker and strain the liquid into a cocktail glass.

For option number 2, garnish with half slice of orange before serving.

frozen apple

This cocktail is best made in a blender. It uses apple brandy and half the white of an egg, which gives it a frothy, frosted finish. The egg is effectively 'cooked' by the alcohol, but you could leave it out, if preferred, or replace it with a dash of orange juice.

Ingredients:

1 good scoop crushed ice

1 measure applejack or Calvados

1 tbsp sugar

2 tsps lime juice

$^1/_2$ the white of 1 egg

Method:

Place the crushed ice in a blender and add the remaining ingredients.

Whizz together until blended, and pour the liquid into a pre-chilled cocktail glass.

steeplejack

This is a lovely, tall drink and very refreshing. It is a cross between the 19th-century fizz and a Collins, but very simple to make, as you will see.

Ingredients:

6 to 8 ice cubes

1 measure applejack

1½ measures chilled apple juice

1½ measures chilled soda water

1 lemon slice

Method:

Fill a highball or Collins glass with ice cubes, pour in the remaining liquid ingredients.

Stir gently and garnish with the lemon slice.

calvados cocktails

big apple

Ingredients:

3 to 4 ice cubes

1 measure apple juice

2 tsps brandy

1 measure applejack

The name 'big apple' is most famously associated with New York, but is also the name of a Jazz Age dance. This drink calls for applejack, which is sometimes known as 'Jersey lightning', after the state in which it is produced.

Method:

Place the ice cubes in a mixing glass and pour in the apple juice, brandy and applejack.

Stir and strain the liquid into a pre-chilled cocktail glass.

Anis Cocktails

'Anis' is used to describe all drinks that are aniseed-flavoured and, more specifically, refers to liqueurs of different degrees of sweetness. The best-known anis drinks are absinthe, pastis, raki (and arak), ouzo (sometimes also called douzico) and sambuca, and there are a number of very well-known proprietary brands, such as Ricard and Pernod. There is also anisette, an aniseed-flavoured liqueur from France, the best-known producer of which is a firm called Marie Brizard.

At around 68 per cent alcohol by volume (abv), absinthe is often called the 'green muse' and the 'green goddess', the former because it was a popular drink among such French Impressionist painters as Degas and Toulouse-Lautrec and their models, and the latter because of its reputed qualities as an aphrodisiac. Although it is often associated with France, absinthe is, in fact, a 'native' of Switzerland.

Absinthe had been banned in most European countries by the beginning of the 20th century on the grounds that it endangered health: its main ingredient, wormwood (*Artemisia absinthium*, which gives the drink its name), was reputed to cause madness and death. Despite the ban, the Swiss continued to produce the drink illegally while, in Spain, it was produced legally. In large doses, wormwood is indeed a hallucinogen, but its detrimental effects on health, beyond excessive alcohol intake, have not, so far, been proven. The ban on absinthe was lifted in recent years, and it is now possible to buy it once again.

Anis drinks of around 45 per cent abv were introduced to replace the banned absinthe. These drinks are typified by Pernod and pastis from Ricard, which replaced the wormwood of absinthe with star anise, the fruit of the evergreen, Chinese star-anise tree. The name 'pastis' is derived from the French word for 'a mixture', being 'a pastiche' of ingredients. Pastis has a slightly stronger liquorice flavour than Pernod; it has a brownish tinge when neat, and is paler than Pernod when diluted with water. Drinks of this type, including ouzo and raki, are commonly diluted with four or five parts of water, over ice, which turns the liquor a milky white. The resulting 'colour' has given Pernod is its nicknames of 'tiger's milk' and the 'green fairy'.

Sambuca (approximately 40 per cent abv) is related to the sweet anis liqueurs of France and Spain, but is drier, and its distinctive ingredient is derived from the elder bush. Anisette (around 30 per cent abv) is quite a different drink altogether. It is a sweet liqueur made by macerating 16 different seeds – including aniseed – fennel, cloves, coriander and other spices and plants, and then blending the maceration with a neutral spirit and sugar syrup.

absinthe suissesse

Although Absinthe and Pernod both have their origins in Switzerland, it is generally thought that this recipe is derived from the French speakers of Louisiana in the US. Orange-flower water is a perfumed, non-alcoholic essence that originated in France and is used in many cocktails, including the ramos fizz of New Orleans.

Ingredients:

4 to 6 ice cubes

$1\frac{1}{2}$ measures absinthe (or Pernod)

2–3 drops anisette

2–3 drops orange-flower water

1 tsp white crème de menthe

1 egg white

Method:

Place the ice in a shaker and pour in the remaining ingredients.

Shake vigorously and strain the liquid into a pre-chilled cocktail glass.

pink pernod

Pernod turns yellowy white when mixed with water. In this drink, however, it turns a perfect pink, thanks to the grenadine, a cordial made from the sweetened juice of the pomegranate, *Punica granatum*.

Ingredients:

3 to 4 ice cubes

³/₄ measure grenadine

³/₄ measure Pernod

chilled ginger ale, as required

Method:

Place some ice cubes in a highball or Collins glass and pour in the grenadine and Pernod.

Stir gently and top with chilled ginger ale. Stir once more before serving.

anis cocktails

hemingway

Ingredients:

1 ¹/₂ measures absinthe

chilled champagne, as required

This cocktail was created by the American novelist Ernest Hemingway, who himself called it 'death in the afternoon' when offering the recipe to *Esquire* magazine, with the instructions to drink three or five slowly!

Method:

Pour the absinthe into the bottom of a pre-chilled champagne flute and pour in chilled champagne until the mix becomes milky.

tour de france

Named after the country's famous bicycle race, this drink appropriately uses two of France's best-loved ingredients: Pernod, whose production in France began in Pontarlier in 1805, and crème de cassis, the blackcurrant liqueur that is a speciality of Dijon.

Ingredients:

I scoop broken ice

I tsp sugar syrup

$^1/_2$ measure crème de cassis

I$^1/_2$ measures Pernod

I measure (or more) chilled lemonade

Method:

Place the broken ice in a rocks glass and pour in the sugar syrup, crème de cassis and Pernod.

Stir and top up with chilled lemonade.

anis cocktails

absinthe cocktail

Ingredients:

3 to 4 ice cubes

$1\frac{1}{2}$ measures absinthe

$\frac{1}{2}$ measure anisette

$\frac{3}{4}$ measure still mineral water

1 tsp sugar syrup

The artist, Toulouse-Lautrec, is said never to have left home without his personal supply of absinthe, which he carried in a long flask concealed inside a hollowed-out walking stick. He is also known to have painted the Parisian scenes that revolved around drinking the 'green fairy'.

Method:

Place some ice cubes in a mixing glass and pour in the remaining ingredients.

Stir and strain the liquid into a pre-chilled liqueur or cocktail glass.

Add 1 teaspoon of maraschino to the above, and you've got an 'absinthe italiano'.

green dragon

This is not the only green dragon that exists in the cocktail world. Others include a version using a gin–kümmel–crème-de-menthe mix, and a more recent champagne-and-Midori combo. This recipe may sound odd, with its inclusion of milk and cream, but you'll be pleasantly surprised by the flavour!

Ingredients:

6 to 8 ice cubes

2 measures Pernod

2 measures milk

2 measures double cream

1 measure sugar syrup

Method:

Place 3 to 4 ice cubes in a shaker and pour in the remaining ingredients.

Shake vigorously and strain the liquid into a large, pre-chilled, wine glass filled with the rest of the ice.

pernod frappé

You can use any liqueur or spirit to make a frappé, which is basically a short drink that is simply poured over crushed ice in the serving glass and served with a short straw and a cherry on a stick. Try serving these in the summer, as an alternative to drinks that are usually served straight up. It makes a pleasant change.

Ingredients:

2 to 3 ice cubes

2 measures Pernod

$^2/_3$ measure anisette

1 scoop crushed ice

1 measure chilled, still mineral water

1 maraschino cherry, to garnish

Method:

Place some ice cubes in a mixing glass and pour in the Pernod and anisette.

Stir and strain the liquid into a champagne saucer filled with crushed ice.

Top up with chilled mineral water to taste and garnish with a maraschino cherry on a stick.

To make a 'tiger's-eye frappé, use $1^3/_4$ measures Pernod and $^1/_2$ measure peppermint schnaps.

anis cocktails

pernod fizz

This is a glorious mix of Pernod and champagne, with a little mandarin juice thrown in.

Method:

Three-quarters fill a good-sized wine glass with broken ice.

Pour in the Pernod and mandarin juice, and top up with chilled champagne.

Garnish the glass with a slice of orange and the cherry.

Eau de Vie Cocktails

In France, the term *eau de vie* ('water of life') is used for all brandies. Any grape brandy is classed as such, but because cognac and armagnac enjoy strict legislation and prestige in France, lesser grape brandies tend to end up overseas. In general, the term 'eaux de vie' applies to any fruit brandy that is colourless and has been aged in glass or pottery – not in wooden barrels. They are also sometimes known as '*alcools blancs*' ('white alcohols'), and have an alcohol content of 38 to 45 per cent.

Among the finest eaux de vie are those produced in the Alsace region bordering France and Germany, in the Black Forest region of Germany and in northern Switzerland. Every type of fruit is used, but the best-known eaux de vie are those made from cherries, such as Kirsch, from plums (small, sour, blue–purple Switzen plums make the dry white Quetsch, while yellow Mirabelle plums make the fine, white eau de vie), from strawberries (fraise) and from raspberries (framboise). Poire William is made from William's pears (also known as Bartlett pears), largely in Switzerland. This eau de vie is unique in that each bottle contains a single pear. The bottles are actually physically attached to the trees, so that a pear grows inside each one. When the pear (and bottle) is picked, the remaining space is filled with a fragrant, pear brandy.

Aquavit is a general name given to the native spirits of Scandinavia, regardless of flavour, although caraway and dill are the most common. Akavit, the spelling common in Denmark, is a neutral spirit distilled from grain and redistilled with flavourings, a little like gin. Danish akavit is said to date from 1846, when a Polish distiller called Isidor Henius set up shop in the Danish town of Aalborg and produced Aalborg Taffel, or 'red Aalborg', after the colour of its label. Akavit is most often served ice cold in small, ice-frosted, shot glasses, but, increasingly, imaginative bartenders are finding that it is a terrific base for new cocktails.

'Schnaps', or 'schnapps', originally derived from the German *schnappen*, which means to swallow or gulp. In Austria, it is often served chilled and neat, and is flavoured with apples and pears (called Obstler), plums or cherries. In Germany, schnaps (spelled with just one 'p') is also often served neat, but is not downed in one. Instead, it is savoured on the tongue! Korn is another type of clear schnaps from German-speaking regions of Europe, and is produced from a variety of grains.

danish dynamite

This cocktail gets it name from the explosive nature of akavit, which was first made by a Polish vodka-distiller called Isidor Henius in 1846. Ideally, the drink should be served very, very chilled.

Ingredients:

3 to 4 ice cubes

1 1/2 measures orange juice

1 measure akavit

2 tsps lime juice

1/2 orange slice

Method:

Place all of the ingredients except the orange slice in a shaker and shake well.

Strain the liquid into a pre-chilled cocktail glass and garnish with the half orange slice.

viking's helmet

This is a gorgeous lime-flavored long drink that uses aquavit and, if possible, Swedish vodka.

Ingredients:

1 ½ measures aquavit

¾ measure vodka

¾ measure lime juice

⅓ measure pineapple syrup

3 measures ginger ale

Method:

Half-fill a highball glass with ice cubes, and pour in the aquavit, vodka, lime juice and pineapple syrup.

Stir well, and top with ginger ale.

eau de vie cocktails

dorchester golden fizz

This cocktail was created by Guilio Morandin at the Dorchester Hotel, in London's Park Lane. While schnaps used to be difficult to get hold of, it is now available in a wide range of flavours for cocktail use. These include apple, peppermint, cinnamon, cherry and blackberry. This cocktail uses peach schnaps.

Ingredients:

8 to 10 ice cubes

1 1/2 tbsps lemon juice

1 tsp sugar syrup

1/2 measure peach schnaps

1 measure white rum

dash of egg white

chilled lemonade, as required

Method:

Place half of the ice in a shaker and pour in the lemon juice, sugar syrup, peach schnaps and white rum.

Add a dash of egg white and shake vigorously to froth up the mix.

Strain the liquid into a highball glass half-filled with the remaining ice.

Top up the drink with chilled lemonade.

WOO WOO

This cocktail was incredibly popular during the 1980s, when peach schnapps became flavor of the month. Then the drink was known as a Teeny-Weeny Woo-Woo.

Ingredients:

ice cubes

1½ measures peach schnapps

1 measure vodka

4 measures cranberry juice

Method:

Place some ice cubes in a shaker and pour in the remaining ingredients.

Shake well and strain into an ice-filled highball glass.

eau de vie cocktails

akatini

Ingredients:

3 to 4 ice cubes

1 dash Noilly Prat

1 1/2 measures Lysholm Linie aquavit

This is a variation on the martini theme, and comes from Lysholm Linie, the makers of Norway's premium aquavit. In an attempt to establish an overseas market, Jorgen B Lysholm, sent some potato spirit to the East Indies in 1805. As happened with madeira, changes in temperature in passing across the equator – the 'line' in the drink's name – vastly improved the flavour of the brew!

Method:

Place the ice cubes in a mixing glass and pour in the Noilly Prat and aquavit.

Stir briefly and strain the liquid into a pre-chilled cocktail glass.

danish mary

This is one of many variations of the famous bloody Mary invented in 1921 by Fernand, 'Pete' Petiot, of Harry's Bar in Paris. This Danish Mary naturally uses akavit. Other versions include German Mary, made with korn and bloody Maria, made with tequila. For the virtuous there is a non-alcoholic version, the virgin Mary.

Ingredients:

3 to 4 ice cubes

$3^1/_2$ measures tomato juice

2 tsps lemon juice

$^3/_4$ measure Danish akavit

freshly ground black pepper

celery salt

2 dashes Worcestershire sauce

1 stick celery

Method:

Place some ice cubes in a shaker and pour in the tomato juice, lemon juice and akavit.

Season to taste with black pepper, celery salt and Worcestershire sauce.

Strain the liquid into a highball or Collins glass, over more ice if you like, and garnish with a celery stick.

For a German Mary, substitute korn or another flavourless schnaps for the akavit.

the viking

By tradition, Lysholm Linie aquavit is aged for four-and-a-half months on a world cruise. The label of each bottle even lists the date of the cruise and the name of the ship! The recipe for this cocktail, courtesy of Lysholm Linie, makes use of tropical fruits that the aquavit passes as it crosses the Equator.

Ingredients:

6 ice cubes

1 measure pineapple juice

1 measure white Curaçao

1 measure Lysholm Linie aquavit

Method:

Place the ice cubes in a shaker and pour over the pineapple juice, white Curaçao and aquavit.

Shake well and strain the liquid into a cocktail glass.

eau de vie cocktails

frozen fuzzy

Ingredients:

1 measure peach schnapps

1/2 measure triple sec/Cointreau

1/2 measure lime juice

1/2 measure grenadine

1 splash lemon-lime soda

ice cubes

1 lime wedge

Save this frozen fuzzy for an especially hot day.

Method:

Place the ingredients in a blender and fill with enough ice to reach the level of the liquid. Blend well.

Pour the drink into a pre-chilled champagne flute and garnish with a wedge of lime.

Bitters & Fortified Wines

The meaning of the word 'bitters' is wide-ranging, and can be used to describe both bitter essences and alcoholic drinks made from roots, flowers, fruits and their peels, macerated in a neutral spirit. Bitters have appetite-stimulating and digestion-promoting qualities.

Among the most famous patented bitters is angostura (45 per cent alcohol by volume, or abv). This were originally made in the town of Angostura, in Venezuela, but is now produced in Trinidad. The recipe was formulated in 1824 by a military doctor, according to a 'secret formula'. The exact recipe continues to remain a closely guarded secret, but it is known that gentian is the most pronounced ingredient, along with extracts of Seville orange peel, angelica, cardamon, cinnamon, cloves, quinine and galagan (*Alpinia officinarum*). Angostura is an indispensable bar staple – with just a few dashes having the capacity to add sweetness to a sour drink and sharpness to a sweet drink. In addition to angostura bitters, there are also Peychaud bitters (Franco–American bitters) and Underberg bitters from Germany, which have been brewed to a secret family recipe since 1846 .

'Bitters' also describes bitter apéritifs and *digestifs* such as Amer Picon (21 per cent abv), from France, and Campari (24 per cent abv), from Italy.

Amaro is the Italian word for bitters, and the term is used to describe the many (over five hundred) patented, bitter liqueurs produced in that country. Amaros, which are usually dark brown in colour, are made from herbs, plants and tree barks, can be diluted and served with ice as apéritifs, or are served neat as *digestifs*.

Fortified wines are ordinary wines that have been fortified using another form of alcohol: port, sherry and vermouth are all examples of a fortified wine. Port (from Portugal) is fortified by adding local brandy during the grape fermentation. Doing so prevents the grapes from fermenting completely, which is how the wine attains its sweetness. Sherry is the English name for the Spanish 'Jerez', a wine that is also fortified with brandy.

Vermouth is flavoured with herbs, barks and plant extracts. Although produced mainly in France and Italy, the word 'vermouth' comes from the German *Wermut*, which means 'wormwood'. Despite its name, none of the health scares that affected absinthe seem to have troubled vermouth.

Cocktail Heaven   195

black tie

Ingredients:

3 measures cold, white Pineau des Charentes

1 ½ measures champagne

1 black grape

This is the perfect chance to use Pineau des Charentes, a ratafia made in the Cognac region of France. Ratafia is not a geographical appellation, but derives from the ancient French practice of concluding a formal agreement, such as a legal transaction, with the Latin words 'rata fiat' (let the deal be settled) and a shared drink – a 'ratifier.'

Method:

Place the ingredients in a pre-chilled wine glass or flute and garnish with a black grape.

Watch the black grape go up and down!

mermaid

The introduction of blue Curaçao during the 1960s saw cocktail bartenders vying with each other to create new recipes that used it. Curaçao takes its name from the Caribbean island that is famed for its small, bitter oranges of the same name. The clear, colourless, orange-flavoured liqueur was originally produced by the Dutch and is now available in a range of vivid hues.

Ingredients:

3 to 4 ice cubes

$^3/_4$ measure sweet, white vermouth

$^3/_4$ measure gin

$^3/_4$ measure blue Curaçao

chilled bitter orange, as required

$^1/_2$ orange slice

1 thin strip lemon peel

Method:

Place the ice cubes in a highball glass and pour in the white vermouth, gin and blue Curaçao.

Stir together, then top up with bitter orange and stir gently once more.

Garnish with an orange slice and a lemon-peel spiral.

bitters & fortified wines

silver campari

According to legend, this red-coloured apéritif was created by Gaspare Campari in the basement of his café-bar in Milan's fashionable Galleria in 1862. It soon became a most fashionable drink. A papal warrant was issued, even, and Campari was consequently served in the Vatican.

Ingredients:

3 to 4 ice cubes

$^3/_4$ measure Campari

$^3/_4$ measure gin

1 measure lemon juice

2 tsps sugar syrup

sparkling white wine or champagne, as required

1 thin strip lemon peel

Method:

Place the ice cubes in a shaker and pour in the Campari, gin, lemon juice and sugar syrup.

Strain the liquid into a champagne flute and top with sparkling wine.

Twist the lemon peel over the drink to release its oil, and then discard it.

Garnish with a mint sprig if desired.

alaska cocktail

Serve this drink well chilled for that
Alaska feel.

Ingredients:

ice cubes

2 dashes orange bitters

1 $\frac{1}{2}$ measures gin

$\frac{3}{4}$ measure yellow
Chartreuse

Method:

Place the ice cubes in a mixing glass and pour in
the remaining ingredients.

Stir and strain into a pre-chilled cocktail glass.

bitters & fortified wines

bahia cocktail

Sherry has a poor image, at best, which means that it is often overlooked as a first choice for drinks. Fortunately, a number of innovative barmen have created some seriously delicious cocktails using sherry. This one is a little spicy with with a sharp tang.

Ingredients:

6 to 8 ice cubes

1 measure medium sherry

1 measure dry vermouth

2 dashes pastis or Pernod

1 dash angostura bitters

1 thin strip lemon peel

Method:

Place plenty of ice in a mixing glass and pour in the remaining ingredients, except for the lemon peel.

Stir, then strain into a pre-chilled cocktail glass.

Twist the lemon peel over the drink to release its oil, then discard it before serving.

the manager's daughter

This heady cocktail uses Dubonnet, France's vermouth-style apéritif. Fortified wine can be traced back to the ancient Egyptians, but the Romans were the first to include wormwood. These wines became popular in Germany during the 16th century (the German word for wormwood is *Wermut*), and later at the French royal court, where their name became vermouth.

Ingredients:

3 to 4 ice cubes

1 measure apple brandy

$1\frac{1}{2}$ measures Dubonnet

4 measures sparkling bitter lemon

1 lemon slice

Method:

Place the ice cubes in a highball glass and pour in the apple brandy and the Dubonnet.

Stir briefly, then top with sparkling bitter lemon.

Garnish the glass with a lemon slice.

port flip

Flips originated in the 17th century, and take their name from the original method of mixing them: they were flipped back and forth from one vessel to another in order to obtain a smooth mix. Today, most flips are made in a shaker, but are no less creamy as a result.

Ingredients:

3 to 4 ice cubes

1 $\frac{1}{2}$ measures port

2 tsps Cognac

1 tsp sugar syrup

1 egg yolk

grated nutmeg, to garnish

Method:

Place the ice cubes in a shaker and pour in all of the ingredients, except for the nutmeg.

Shake firmly and strain into a champagne flute.

Sprinkle a little grated nutmeg over the top.

bitters & fortified wines

southern tango

The 'southern' aspect of this cocktail comes from the inclusion of America's strong, dry, bourbon-and-peach liqueur, Southern Comfort. Here, it accompanies a pale-golden, dry vermouth, traditionally aged in oak vats.

Ingredients:

1 scoop broken ice

1 measure dry vermouth

$1/2$ measure Southern Comfort

2 measures chilled lemonade

Method:

Two-thirds fill a highball glass with broken ice, and pour in the vermouth and Southern Comfort.

Top with chilled lemonade to serve.

Mocktails

Alcohol is not for everybody, whether on medical or dietary grounds, or because of religious beliefs. Some people on a night out may be driving or may be under age, while others simply don't like the taste of alcohol. Some may be allergic to alcohol, they might be 'in recovery' or they might just not want a drink at that moment. Whatever the reasons, if someone says 'no thanks' to a cocktail, then don't press one on them. There are lots of wonderful-tasting and good-looking 'mocktails' to be offered instead.

Of the hundreds of delicious mocktails to be enjoyed, some were specially designed, others, like the virgin Mary (a bloody Mary without the vodka) a virgin colada (a piña colada without the rum) or a virgin bellini (a bellini without the champagne) are non-alcoholic alternatives to famous cocktails and are very easy to make.

If you serve mocktails, they should look just as appealing as their alcoholic cousins. Take the same care over ingredients and the same time and effort over their presentation. With many mixed drinks, mocktails included, it's almost impossible to tell whether there is alcohol in them or not just by looking at them. If you're providing drinks for a number of people, make sure you know your ingredients. Read the labels on the bottles: many so-called 'non-alcoholic' beers do, in fact, contain a small amount of alcohol. Adding a dash of bitters to a glass of tonic water also means you've added alcohol, even if it is only a very tiny amount.

Many of the recipes in this section are also ideal for children to make – they are so easy. Kids are entranced by the bright colours, crazy names, the mixing and, above all, the decorative bits and swizzle sticks associated with cocktails. Why not let them create a few drinks of their own? Fruity drinks are certainly more healthy than sugar-filled, fizzy concoctions. By using 'diet' versions of cola and lemonade, you will reduce the sugar intake if that is something that concerns you. It might also be sensible to invest in some clear plastic beakers rather than using your finest cocktail glasses, and make sure you have plenty of straws and umbrellas!

mocktails

virgin bellini

Ingredients:

3 measures peach nectar

1 teaspoon grenadine

1 measure lemon juice

4 measures chilled soda water

This cocktail can be made either by using peach nectar or by 'crushing' a peeled and pitted peach in a blender.

Method:

Pour the peach nectar into a pre-chilled champagne flute.

Add the grenadine and lemon juice and top with the chilled soda water.

Stir well.

mickey mouse

This is possibly more an ice-cream float than a mocktail, but if you a) can remember all of the words to the Mickey Mouse Club song; or b) ever had a Mouseketeer's hat with your name on it, you have every right to thoroughly enjoy this!

Ingredients:

5 measures cold cola

1 scoop vanilla (or your favourite flavour) ice cream

1 measure whipped cream

2 maraschino cherries

grated chocolate

Method:

Pour the cold cola into a highball glass and float the ice cream on top.

Spoon on the whipped cream and garnish with the two cherries. Dust liberally with grated chocolate before serving.

mocktails

rail splitter

Dating from the US Prohibition era, this cocktail would have made a refreshing railroad cooler.

Ingredients:

ice cubes

1 measure lemon juice

¾ measure gomme syrup

4 measures ginger ale

Method:

Place the ice cubes in a highball glass and pour in the lemon juice and gomme syrup.

Top up with ginger ale and stir.

Garnish the glass with a spiral of lemon peel.

brontosaurus

Here's a long, low-calorie drink to enjoy as the sun goes down. The celery-stick garnish is a tribute to the herbivorous diet of the mocktail's long-extinct namesake.

Ingredients:

ice cubes

3 measures grapefruit juice

$\frac{1}{2}$ measure lime juice

$\frac{1}{2}$ measure grenadine

3 measures lemonade

1 stick celery

Method:

Half-fill a shaker with ice cubes and pour in the grapefruit juice, lime juice and grenadine.

Shake well and strain the liquid into an ice-filled highball glass.

Top up with lemonade and garnish with a celery stick (optional).

mocktails

mocktails

bora-bora

Ingredients:

ice cubes

3 measures pineapple juice

1 teaspoon lime juice

1/2 measure grenadine

3 measures dry ginger ale

1 lime slice

1 maraschino cherry

Bora-Bora is in the Society Islands, part of French Polynesia in the Pacific Ocean, northwest of Tahiti. As you drink this pineapple-flavour mocktail, it will not take much to conjure up images of swaying palm trees and tropical beaches.

Method:

Half-fill a shaker with ice cubes and pour in the pineapple juice, lime juice and grenadine.

Shake well and strain the liquid into an ice- filled glass.

Top with the ginger ale and garnish with a slice of lime and a cherry.

st. clements

Ingredients:

broken ice

2 measures orange juice

2 measures sparkling bitter lemon

I orange slice

I lemon and lime slice

'Oranges and lemons, say the bells of St Clement's'.

Method:

Two-thirds fill a highball glass with broken ice.

Pour in the orange juice and add the sparkling bitter lemon.

Garnish the glass with the orange and lemon and lime slices and serve with straws.

prohibition punch

Prohibition punch makes a great non-alcoholic party drink, especially if you have plenty of guests and it's a mixed crowd. This recipe makes about six glasses.

Ingredients:

ice cubes

3 measures lemon juice

225ml ($\frac{1}{2}$ pint) apple juice

1 measure gomme syrup

500ml (1 pint) ginger ale

orange slices

Method:

Place some ice cubes in a jug or pitcher and pour in the lemon juice, apple juice and gomme syrup.

Stir gently and pour in the ginger ale.

Serve in ice-filled highball glasses, garnishing each with an orange slice.

mocktails

tail feathers

Here is a long, refreshing, ginger-beer based drink from America's Prohibition era.

Ingredients:

ice cubes

1 measure orange juice

5 measures ginger beer

(not ginger ale)

1 sprig mint

Method:

Place the ice cubes in a highball glass and pour in the orange juice and ginger beer.

Garnish the drink with a sprig of mint.

shirley temple

A number of mixed drinks and cocktails have been named after celebrities, among them the novelist Ernest Hemingway, actresses Rosalind Russell and Marjorie King (the Margarita), artist Charles Gibson and the millionaire Colonel Cornelius Vanderbilt. In some circles, all mocktails are called 'Shirley Temples' after the child star. For purists (and film buffs), however, there is, and only ever will be, one Shirley Temple.

Ingredients:

ice cubes (if served in a highball)

5 measures cold lemon-lime soda or 5 measures cold ginger ale

1 teaspoon grenadine

Method:

For a champagne saucer, fill the pre-chilled saucer with cold lemon-lime soda or ginger ale.

Add the grenadine and garnish with a cherry and orange slice, if desired.

For a highball, place some ice cubes in the glass, pour in the lemon-lime soda or ginger ale, and add the grenadine. Stir well and garnish with a cherry and orange slice if desired.

mocktails

mocktails

southern ginger

This southern ginger is a non-alcoholic version of the mint julep.

Ingredients:

2 sprigs of mint

broken ice

1/2 measure lemon juice

1/2 measure gomme syrup

5 measures dry ginger ale

Method:

Place one sprig of mint in a highball glass and gently crush it to squeeze out some juice.

Two-thirds fill the glass with broken ice and pour in the lemon juice, gomme syrup and ginger ale.

Mix gently, then garnish with the remaining sprig of mint.

roy rogers

This popular mocktail is named after Hollywood's most famous singing cowboy.

Ingredients:

ice cubes

4 measures ginger ale

2 measures lemon-lime soda

1 teaspoon grenadine

Method:

Place some ice cubes in a highball glass and pour in the ginger ale, lemon-lime soda and grenadine.

Stir well and garnish with a cherry and orange slice, if desired.

mocktails

pink lemonade

This is a very easy drink to make, and one where you can adjust the measures to suit your taste.

Ingredients:

ice cubes

1 1/2 measures lemon juice

1 1/2 measures gomme syrup

1/3 measure grenadine

4 measures ice-cold water

1 orange wedge

1 cherry

Method:

Half-fill a shaker with ice cubes.

Pour in the lemon juice, gomme syrup, grenadine and water and shake well.

Strain the liquid into an ice-filled highball glass and garnish with an orange wedge and a cherry.

pomola

The pomola is very easy to put together and makes a welcome change from a 'straight' iced cola.

Ingredients:

ice cubes

5 measures cold cola

1 measure lime juice

$^1/_3$ measure grenadine

1 slice lime

Method:

Place some ice cubes in a highball glass.

Pour in the cold cola, the lime juice and the grenadine.

Stir gently and garnish with a slice of lime.

cranberry refresher

This thirst-quenching mocktail has a lovely colour and a fresh, dry taste.

Ingredients:

ice cubes

4 measures cranberry juice

2 measures red grape juice

2 measures lemon-lime soda

Method:

Place some ice cubes in a highball glass and pour in the cranberry juice and red grape juice.

Top with lemon-lime soda and stir well.

Garnish with a lime wedge, if desired.

mocktails

Index

Index

Index